LEARN'NG IN THE WORKPLACE

D1419119

For ALJ and HGB

Learning in the workplace

Strategies for effective practice

Stephen Billett

ALLEN & UNWIN

Allen & Unwin
83 Alexander Street
Crows Nest NSW 2065
Australia
Phone: (61 2) 8425 0100
Fax: (61 2) 9906 2218
Email: frontdesk@allen-unwin.com.au
Web: http://www.allenandunwin.com

National Library of Australia
Cataloguing-in-Publication entry:

Billet, Stephen.
    Learning in the workplace: strategies for effective practice.

    Bibliography.
    Includes index.
    ISBN 1 86508 364 X.

    1. Occupational training. 2. Employees – Training of. I. Title.

658.3124

Set in 10/13pt Caslon540 by Midland Typesetters, Maryborough, Victoria
Printed by CMO Image Printing Enterprise, Singapore

10 9 8 7 6 5 4 3 2 1

Foreword

We often think of learning as the province of schools and colleges, as the outcome of teaching. We have all experienced life as students in the classroom and have often come to associate learning with what those places do. This is a misleading perception which can draw attention away from where learning really happens. Most of our learning did not occur there even when we were young; it certainly does not happen there in working life.

The workplace was once seen as a place to work, to produce goods or offer services. It was not the place to learn. Learning occurred before employment or as part of an apprenticeship or special training period. The demands of work have now become more complex. No amount of initial training can prepare someone for a lifetime of work. Jobs change, new technologies emerge, new opportunities are created. All this requires learning, and relearning.

Learning is in fact a normal human process that occurs throughout life, prompted by the events and challenges of everyday existence. It occurs everywhere. We all do it, all the time. We do it in the home, during leisure and at work. Only a small proportion of the learning in which we engage happens in classrooms or in conjunction with a formal course of study.

There has been a revolution in thinking over the past twenty years or so. In educational institutions the focus has moved decisively from teaching to learning. It has taken a long time to acknowledge that learning is everywhere. But now we are seeing an explosion of interest in the learning that takes place in adult life. Nowhere is this more true than in learning at work.

When learning was seen as the responsibility of teachers, the focus of research on teaching and learning was on what they did to foster it. Now that has begun to shift, research is taking place on what managers, supervisors and co-workers can do to help, how workplaces can be organised to promote the kinds of learning needed there and, indeed, on what employees can do to assist their own learning. This research is relatively new and it has yet to make a significant impact on working life.

Stephen Billett's book is therefore particularly timely. It is the first to take the increasingly large body of new research and thinking about work and learning and make it generally accessible. In particular, the book makes this knowledge available in ways that allow it to make an impact on how work is organised and structured. In discussing what he calls 'a curriculum for the workplace', the book shows how ideas about guided learning can be implemented in real settings. When applied in organisations, such rethinking of learning in work can be used to improve both productivity and the quality of working life.

The book is a revelation for those who may not be aware of the many recent studies illuminating learning at work. There are large number of examples from very diverse industries: from coal mining to hairdressing and from information technology to manufacturing. Although I have written in this area myself, I was surprised and delighted to see how Stephen Billett has drawn on so many interesting cases in so many settings. He has provided a sense of the richness and complexity of learning at work, while providing useful ways of looking at what can be done to positively influence it.

He writes as a leading researcher whose work has been internationally recognised and who has undertaken research on learning in many different workplaces. Unlike others, this book is not a prescription for a 'quick fit' for workplace problems. It provides practical

solutions but in ways that enable readers to understand the issues
involved and appreciate what might be needed in situations different
to those described. The reader is stimulated to think through the
implications of the important ideas that are lucidly discussed here
and apply them in their own context.

Learning in the workplace has come of age with the publication
of this book. It shows the way for a new level of sophistication in
the ways learning and work are treated. It is respectful of the challenges of very many different types that are faced. And it opens new
territory for exploration in the world of learning throughout life.

David Boud
Professor of Adult Education
University of Technology, Sydney

Contents

Tables and figures

TABLES

FIGURES

Glossary

Accommodation Modification of existing cognitive structures when encountering a new task or stimulus that results in the development of new knowledge (categories or subsystems). A source of refinement to cognitive structures that does not abolish the established knowledge structures but differentiates them by introducing a new subsystem or category (Piaget 1976).

Appropriation The use of interpretative constructing knowledge derived from a social source which the individual 'makes their own'. Wertsch (1998) contrasts appropriation—when individuals construct meaning empathetically—with mastery—reproducing some behaviour to which the individual is not wholly committed.

Assimilation Understanding a task or stimulus through the application of existing categories of knowledge. It involves incorporating task requirements or stimuli into existing knowledge structures (categories or subsystems) (Piaget 1966).

Automisation Any procedure that can be performed automatically without conscious thought, through a process of repeated rehearsal or practice as in proceduralisation (compilation and composition).

Chunking Developing associations between concepts to secure almost instantaneous categorisation of and response to tasks (Pea 1993); premised on the development of links between concepts (e.g. red = stop; green = go) until the use of one readily triggers the other.

Coaching Guidance and monitoring by a more experienced coworker or expert of learners conducting work activities. The provision of hints, feedback and clues, as well as demonstrating, modelling and explaining 'tricks of the trade' can assist the development and refinement of workplace procedures through coaching.

Co-construction A reciprocal process of knowledge construction in which the object (the source) and the subject (the learner) are both transformed (Valsiner 1994). The learner constructs a view of the source of knowledge as much as of the knowledge itself, making judgments about the veracity of both.

Cognitive structures From the cognitive view, the representations of conceptual and procedural knowledge in memory deployed in thinking and acting, which are themselves developed further as a consequence of thinking and acting.

Compilation Changes from a declarative or stateable form of knowledge to procedural representations of knowledge that can be performed without conscious thought.

Composition The collapsing of a series of compiled procedures into a single, smooth procedure (e.g. the procedures required to change gears in a car).

Conceptual knowledge (also referred to as declarative knowledge) Comprises facts, information, propositions, assertions and concepts. Levels comprising stateable facts and concepts of increasing depth (complexity premised on associations) differentiate conceptual knowledge.

Deep conceptual knowledge Premised on links, associations and relations among concepts (Prawat 1989). It is required to successfully complete non-routine tasks, such as the transfer of knowledge or addressing a novel problem, and the monitoring of performance.

Direct guidance Direct interactions between experts or more experienced coworkers and learners that are focused on developing knowledge collaboratively through joint problem-solving. Particularly important for learning that would not occur unaided.

Dispositions   Comprise attitudes, values, affect, interests and identities (Prawat 1989). Perkins et al. (1993) regard dispositions as individuals' tendencies to put their capabilities into action. Dispositions underpin concepts and procedures, and are sourced through individuals' personal histories and other social practices such as work.

Equilibrium   Individuals' need to integrate new information with what they already know (i.e. their existing knowledge structures) through the processes of assimilation and accommodation (Piaget 1966) in order to overcome dis-equilibrium, thereby maintaining viability with what is experienced (von Glasersfeld 1987).

Expertise   The ability to perform tasks that are both routine and non-routine activities within a domain of knowledge. In particular, expertise is the ability to perform effectively non-routine tasks within a vocation that might reasonably be expected from a skilled vocational practitioner.

Fading   The gradual removal of support from experts or coworkers until learners can independently and proficiently perform tasks.

Guided learning   The process of collaborative learning through which more experienced others aid learners through joint problem-solving and pressing the learners into thinking and acting, rather than teaching them didactically.

Indirect guidance   Contributions to learning in the form of guidance arising from indirect (distal) interactions with the social and physical environment. Observing and listening to other workers are examples of indirect guidance, as is the ability to view artefacts and tools in the workplace.

Knowledge   From a cognitive perspective, the conceptual, procedural and dispositional representation of knowledge we hold and organise in memory.

Learning   The process of constructing new knowledge, its ongoing reinforcement and enhancing its breadth and organisation through deployment. Analogous to problem-solving of both non-routine (new) or non-routine (reinforcing) kinds.

Microgenetic development The moment-by-moment learning that constantly occurs through our ongoing thinking and acting and which we use to construct and reinforce our knowledge (Rogoff 1995).

Modelling The process by which the expert executes a task with learners engaging in building a conceptual model of the task, its goals, subgoals and outcome through observation.

New knowledge Extending and transforming existing knowledge structures, such as in non-routine problem-solving or through accommodation.

Pedagogy Broadly referred to as the science and art of teaching, but often used to describe an approach to how learning should proceed and the consequences of that approach.

Procedural knowledge Comprises techniques, skills and the ability to secure goals (Anderson 1982); has been classified into levels or orders (Stevenson 1991) from specific procedures—those we use to perform routine tasks seemingly unconsciously—through to higher order procedures—those which monitor performance and perform an executive role in how we direct our thinking.

Readiness Piagetian term for the preparedness of the individual to respond to a particular task—for instance, having the level of knowledge and/or appropriate disposition required to learn a particular task.

Reinforcement Events and interactions that strengthen the links between particular activities and responses. It comprises either intrinsic reinforcement—from within the individual (e.g. satisfaction with overcoming a problem; a sense of viability) or from outside (e.g. supportive comments from a peer)—that informs about task performance.

Rich learning Learning that is enriched by its scope and organisation, which assists its subsequent deployment.

Robust knowledge Vocational knowledge that offers the prospect of transfer across situations and circumstances in which the vocation is practised.

Scaffolding   Provides learners with opportunities to acquire knowledge and skills by monitoring their performance in tasks that are within their scope of learning. As Brown and Palinscar (1989: 411) state, the 'metaphor of a scaffold captures the idea of an adjustable and temporary support that can be removed when no longer necessary'.

Transfer   Applying knowledge to a situation or circumstance that is different from the one in which it is constructed. 'Near' transfer is the ability to apply the knowledge to something quite similar to what is already known. 'Far' transfer is the application of knowledge to circumstances that are different from those in which the knowledge was first learnt.

Viability   The drive to maintain equilibrium in the face of new experiences and stimuli (von Glasersfeld 1987).

Vocational college   An educational institution that focuses on the development of outcomes specific to a particular vocation or occupation.

Introduction

The only adequate training for occupations is training through occupations.

(Dewey 1916: 310)

... learning is ubiquitous in on-going activity, though often unrecognized as such.

(Lave 1993: 5)

WORKPLACE LEARNING: INTEREST AND AMBIVALENCE

My interest in workplace learning began in the early 1990s, when I started to consider the role it played in developing employees' ability to perform at work. At that time, I was involved in encouraging enterprises to participate in structured vocational education programs. This was part of a national reform process to improve the effectiveness of workers' skills in order to compete globally. This task took me to numerous enterprises, where I observed many work practices and talked with a wide range of workers about their work and how they learnt it. Through these experiences, two consistent issues arose.

1

Firstly, many of these workers had not been prepared for their work through vocational educational programs. This was because such programs were either unavailable or inappropriate for their type of work. Instead, they had learnt their vocational practice through working. Secondly, they did not seem to be any the worse for this kind of preparation. The workplace-based preparation seemed to have equipped them well for their work roles.

These conclusions came together one day in a small sugar mill town. A sugar mill in full production during the 'crush' is a spectacular sight. During this period, the production workers monitor and make adjustments to the production process in order to maximise the yield from the cane. But how did the workers learn these complex and demanding skills? I knew that there was little movement of workers between the various towns and mills. There was also no formalised training for the milling operations. This meant that the knowledge required to operate the mill resided largely within it and the surrounding community. Learning processes that were part of everyday work practices had assisted these workers to understand and successfully operate the mill. This realisation led to a questioning of my assumptions about how learning for vocations proceeds. I had been a college-trained technician, who had become a vocational educator through a teaching training college and had subsequently been involved in the professional development of teachers, supported by university studies. Hence I had come to associate rich learning—legitimately structured and transferable knowledge—with teaching. However, in many workplaces—such as the sugar mills and coal mines I had visited—there was evidence of learning that challenged this assumption. This led me to attempt to understand how and what individuals learn through everyday activity in the workplace, the strengths and weaknesses of that learning and how it might be improved.

The last decade has seen a growth of interest in workplaces as environments for learning vocational practice. This interest can be found within governments and enterprises, the professions and trades, and also in individuals who wish to gain vocational knowledge (Boud & Garrick 1999). However, there persists a deeply rooted ambivalence towards learning in workplaces. On the one hand, there is a valuing of the authentic experiences that workplaces provide for the development of the vocational knowledge needed for work. On the other hand, workplaces are characterised as being 'informal' learning environments that fail to provide coherence in the structuring of learning experiences, are devoid of access to instructional episodes and lead to piecemeal, concrete and situationally specific learning outcomes.

Some of this ambivalence can be explained by different and sometimes conflicting purposes of government, industry and enterprises. Governments express the least ambivalence, especially for some areas of work. Their goals are often focused on making the content of vocational education programs relevant to industry and directly applicable within enterprises. Through this, they aim to engage enterprise support for and sponsorship of these programs. Hence, for government, a focus on work as a medium for learning is proposed as addressing perceived concerns about the relevance of vocational education programs based within educational institutions. Also, for government, learning within workplaces brings the prospect of transferring from the public to the private purse some of the cost of developing vocational skills. If the development occurs in workplaces rather than publicly funded vocational colleges, the costs to government can be reduced. Enterprise interest in workplace learning is usually associated with enhancing employees' access to skill development that is directly relevant to the enterprise's specific needs—and in ways that can also contain costs. Teachers are interested in their students engaging in workplace experiences to assist the transfer of learning from classrooms to other situations. In this context, workplace experiences are often intended to make learning in educational institutions relevant and applicable to what is required in the workplace (Hamilton & Hamilton 1997; Stasz & Kaganoff 1997; Stasz & Brewer 1999). However, the focus is usually on workplace experiences supporting the goals of the educational institution's programs—that is, assisting the transfer of classroom-learnt knowledge in a way that is consistent with the goals of the educational programs.

For the trades and professions, there is nothing new about learning through work, nor about the ambivalence towards it.

Apprenticeship programs leading to trade recognition and internships for the major professions (law, medicine and accounting) have long demanded extensive periods of workplace practice prior to admission to the trade or profession. However, these experiences are only legitimated through their integration within, or because they follow on from, courses in educational institutions. On their own, workplace experiences would not be sufficient for admission to the professions and are resisted in the trades. Vocational education students are also attracted to the authenticity of workplace experiences and the prospect of securing employable vocational knowledge through these experiences. However, students also express concern that what they learn in a particular workplace may not be transferable to others, or may not be widely acknowledged when certification is enterprise-based (Billett & Hayes 1999).

Taken together, these interests reflect the ambivalence directed towards workplace learning. There is acknowledgment of the relevance and utility of workplace experiences in learning and developing further vocational practice. There are also pragmatic interests associated with the focus, cost and access to skill development of workplace learning. Yet concerns persist about the legitimacy and structuring of workplace learning experiences and the specificity and quality of outcomes. Overall, the most consistent interest is in the unique contributions of workplaces that are simply not available elsewhere. However, despite this interest, there is limited evidence that workplaces have been seen as legitimate learning settings in their own right (Boud 1998). Workplace experiences are viewed by key advocates (the trades, professions and educators) principally as a means to apply and refine what has been learnt in educational institutions or as 'fallback' settings when these institutions lack the expertise or infrastructure to provide appropriate learning experiences. This supports the assumption that, rather than just being of a different kind, learning experiences in workplaces are inherently less valuable than those in educational institutions. Undercutting such an assumption is a body of research (e.g. Raizen 1994) that suggests learning in educational institutions is often fragile—that it is not readily transferable to other settings, such as workplaces. Ironically, it is to workplace experiences that researchers have looked to improve the transferability of knowledge learnt in these institutions (e.g. Collins et al. 1989; Brown et al. 1989; Raizen 1994).

In order to understand more fully the contributions of workplaces, and to reconcile some of the ambivalence towards them, a comprehensive view of their contributions to learning vocational practice needs to be developed and articulated. A pedagogy for the workplace is warranted, including a workplace curriculum. This pedagogy should aim to guide practice, and to assist in conceptualising instruction and curriculum practice to support learning in workplaces. For learning in workplaces to be viewed as worthwhile in its own right, this pedagogy needs to articulate how the long-valued contributions of workplace experiences can best be utilised. The ways in which workplace experiences contribute to successful performance at work must be identified, along with the ability to transfer that performance to new tasks and to situations beyond the one in which it was learnt. Through an analysis of the process of learning, this book identifies and appraises the requirements of vocational practice, the strengths and weaknesses of learning vocational practice through work, and the contributions of workplaces as learning environments. To understand how these environments can best assist and support the development of transferable vocational practice, it also identifies approaches to organising and assisting learning in workplaces. This outcome is important for workers as learners, for the enterprises that employ skilful workers and for national goals of maintaining and developing levels of economic performance.

A model of workplace curriculum is proposed, founded in the contributions of activities and guidance as part of everyday work practice. This curriculum aims to assist those wishing to learn about and develop further their vocational practice through participation in work. For many workers, such as the sugar mill workers, no option exists other than to develop this knowledge in the workplace. Such is their specialisation that no courses currently exist—or are ever likely to be viable—through either public or private provisions of vocational education. Consequently, workplaces are the most promising—and perhaps the only—locations in which it is possible to learn and further develop such vocational expertise. More broadly, the growing need for continuous learning to maintain and develop individuals' vocational practice throughout their working life (Candy & Matthews 1998) can perhaps best be addressed in workplace settings. However, it is also necessary to address legitimate concerns about learning in an environment where the central activity and focus are not explicitly upon individuals' development. Importantly, the focus of this book is not directly training in the workplace *per se*. Instead, it focuses on how people learn through their everyday work, and how workplaces and workplace experiences contribute to their learning. It also examines how learning for vocational practice might be improved.

KEY PREMISES

Five key premises are proposed in presenting a case for a pedagogy for the workplace and a workplace curriculum. First, learning is taken as something that occurs as part of everyday thinking and acting. It is not reserved for the classroom or the training room; it is ongoing in our everyday experiences. If we are thinking and acting, we are learning.

Second, rather than being premised on the instructional and curriculum practices of educational institutions, a workplace curriculum needs to be founded on the contributions and circumstances afforded by workplace environments. Within this book, assumptions about relationships between teaching and learning are questioned and distinctions drawn between experiences in classrooms and those in workplaces. This questioning is not intended as a criticism of educational institutions or teachers' work. Rather, as with other approaches to structuring learning outside of educational institutions (e.g. distance and Web-based educational provisions), it asks vocational educators to consider how their practice can be reconstituted to assist the learning of vocational practice in workplaces. Furthermore, such questioning is intended as a device to test assumptions about learning more generally. Distinctions are made between the different kinds of experiences and guidance provided in both workplaces and educational institutions. This is largely because the goals, activities undertaken and guidance provided are of different kinds. Further, different—but not necessarily qualitatively inferior—outcomes are likely to be realised from the experiences provided in each of these two settings.

Third, it is inadequate to believe that learning simply by 'just doing it' will suffice. There are clear limitations to learning in workplaces as part of everyday work. These are more obvious when access to appropriate guidance and support is lacking. You only have to experience the services and products of those who lack adequate preparation to understand these shortcomings. There are also consequences for individuals' learning when access to sources of understanding and guidance is limited or simply unavailable. Skilled workers have to respond to new tasks in the workplace and transfer their vocational practice to other situations. Consequently, workplace learning experiences need to be structured to develop this capacity in workers.

Fourth, workplaces are contested terrain. This contestation manifests itself in relationships between workers and management, within and between work teams, in the division of labour and among affiliated groups in the workplace. There are also divisions premised on gender, age, affiliation, bases for employment and ethnicity. Contestation can result in the inequitable distribution of opportunities for learning vocational practice. Certainly, not all interests will be aligned to assist learners to develop their vocational practice. In some cases, there are quite legitimate concerns about displacement by experienced workers. Workplace factors such as these influence individuals' access to activities and guidance—the very bases for learning in workplaces.

Finally, the ideas in this book are not meant to deny the important contribution to the development of vocational knowledge provided by educational institutions. Perhaps the most desirable form of initial preparation for the vocations and their further development is through the kinds of integrated experiences enjoyed by apprentices. This is most potent when the contributions of the school, college or university-based and workplace-based components are complementary. It is anticipated that the ideas presented in this book may be used in such situations to enrich the on-the-job preparation for integrated programs such as those enjoyed by the trades and professions in many countries. In addition, they may provide a basis for the work placement experiences of high school students to be enriched.

The principal audience for this book comprises those who are interested in learning in and for the workplace. This includes those working in human resource development roles, those who are interested in facilitating workplace learning and those whose tertiary studies or research interests are directed towards learning as part of work. Also, the book will be of more than general interest to those working or studying in the fields of adult learning and human resource development. Issues related to lifelong learning, the learning organisation and adult learning are referred to throughout. Principles of instructional design and curriculum development, as they relate to adults learning for work, are also described and illustrated. For instance, those responsible for apprenticeships in the workplace, organising mentoring arrangements in the workplace and integrating school-based learners' experiences of workplaces will find principles to guide workplace learning experiences.

The intention is for this text to present a case that can inform practice. The key goal is to advance an evidence-based model of curriculum to develop vocational expertise through workplace-based experiences. Evidence is drawn from recent investigations of learning at and for work. To meet the needs of a broad audience, illustrations and examples are used to communicate theoretical ideas. These ideas are not always explicitly stated. However, they are brought forward where appropriate to support the argument being advanced. Overall, the presentation aims to make the key premises and propositions accessible to a broad audience interested in work-based learning.

STRUCTURE OF THE BOOK

The book is structured into two parts. Part I aims to develop an understanding of workplaces as learning environments, including their strengths and weaknesses. It comprises three chapters. Chapter 1 explains and illustrates the idea of learning as part of everyday thinking and acting in the workplace. Chapter 2 focuses on the knowledge required for performance at work, which is the goal for workplace learning—one against which its strengths and weaknesses can be judged. Drawing on a program of investigations of learning in workplaces, Chapter 3 evaluates these learning environments. It proposes that workplace experiences provide opportunities for learning new knowledge and the reinforcement of that learning through everyday activities, the guidance of more experienced or expert others and the structuring of experiences that permit movement towards expertise. It also identifies the limitations of everyday learning in the workplace. So, while the contributions of workplace learning are identified as attributes that need to be fully utilised, the limitations represent shortcomings, the impact of which needs to be eliminated or diminished through particular kinds of interventions.

Part II focuses on delineating a curriculum for the workplace. It also comprises three chapters. Chapter 4 advances a model of workplace curriculum which proposes a pathway of guided participation in workplace activities, taking the learner from being a novice to an expert, supported by the direct guidance of more experienced others, the indirect guidance of other workers and the contributions of the physical environment. Together, these experiences constitute the first of three levels of guidance available in the workplace. Given the significance of guidance by more experienced coworkers, it is necessary to elaborate on the contributions of guided learning at work. This is the focus of Chapter 5, which details how the direct guidance of more experienced coworkers augments what is provided freely by the workplace. It focuses on how guided learning can strengthen the contributions of everyday participation at work. In doing so, it elaborates two further levels of guided learning: the use of strategies to secure immediate performance and the learning associated with realising more strategic and transferable learning outcomes. Chapter 6 identifies and discusses the role of the enterprise in organising and managing workplace learning arrangements.

PART I

Understanding workplaces as learning environments

1

Working and learning

WORKPLACES AS LEARNING ENVIRONMENTS

The two production workers had spent most of the morning trying to free a chute that had become blocked with a build up of 'fines'—tiny particles of ore. They worked together, discussing the problem and communicating constantly with the control room as they tried different means of removing the blockage and adjusting the feed from the conveyor belt to prevent it happening again. As they worked on the problem, another worker—a new employee—was listening to the exchanges between the control room and the fitters on his 'two-way'. Once the blockage had been cleared and the belts and feeders to the kilns were operating again, the two workers continued to adjust the feed from the conveyors, still communicating with the control room workers. The new worker continued to listen.

Through their actions, all those involved had extended their understanding of the plant and the best means of controlling the flow of the ore. They had done this through participation in an everyday work activity. In the process, they had received feedback from colleagues about the effectiveness of the various settings they had used. The control room workers had applied their knowledge of the plant in a different way from their usual monitoring and control activities, and learnt more about how feed adjustments affect the flow of the ore. The new employee who had been following the procedures had built a mental model of what the other workers had been doing. Later, over lunch, this novice listened in as the two production workers discussed with others the adjustments they had made, thereby extending his understanding of the procedures used.

Through their engagement in different kinds of workplace activities and the guidance provided by other workers, these workers had learnt more about their vocational practice, extending their understanding of and procedural ability required for their work. This learning occurred through everyday work activity. For the novice, the learning was of a different order, relating to the kinds of task goals to be achieved and the means of achieving these goals. This could have included such things as the relationships among the particular functions of this part of the processing plant, the quality of the ore and control of the flow of the ore.

As the above vignette illustrates, workplaces structure and routinely provide learning experiences as part of everyday work activities and through guidance from other workers. Participation in workplace tasks assists new learning and reinforces what has been learnt through further practice. This account of the workplace's contributions to learning is consistent with contemporary learning theories, which helps substantiate the case for workplaces to be seen as legitimate and effective learning environments. This legitimisation is important as there remains much scepticism about the quality of learning acquired in workplaces. An explanation of how situational contributions to learning influence the way individuals learn their vocational practice is part of this legitimisation.

The common labelling of workplaces as 'informal' learning environments reveals their ambiguous status in terms of learning. Even advocates have described workplace learning processes and outcomes as being 'informal' and 'incidental', and as failing to furnish critical insights (Marsick & Watkins 1990). Although unintended, this labelling has fostered a view that learning experiences in the workplace are incoherent, lack structure and have outcomes wholly specific to the particular enterprise. The use of negative labels for workplace learning, such as 'non-formal' and 'informal', persists— usually without critical appraisal. Perhaps it is not surprising, given the pervasiveness of most individuals' encounters with educational institutions, that views about the qualities of workplace learning will commonly be based on what happens in these institutions.

Teaching and learning are often seen to be synonymous, so the absence of qualified teachers and a deliberately structured curriculum can easily lead to assumptions that learning in workplaces will be inferior to that occurring in schools, colleges and universities. Workplace learning may be seen as piecemeal because the activities are not structured in ways consistent with the familiar organisation of learning experiences adopted in educational institutions. Accordingly, weak or incidental learning outcomes will be anticipated wherever personnel in the workplace lack formal instructional expertise. In this view, which privileges the practices of educational institutions, the absence of a written curriculum, qualified teachers and the teaching practices found in educational institutions raises the concern that learning in workplaces—if it occurs at all—will be weak, piecemeal, concrete and incidental.

However, many of these premises are questionable. Although not written down, the pathways of experience and guidance provided in workplaces are often structured or 'formalised'. Just as the goals and practices of educational institutions frame the activities in which students engage, so too the goals and practices of workplaces determine workplace activities (Billett 1996a; Scribner 1997). Further, rather than being weak, the learning occurring outside teaching and institutional practice is often central to sustaining the practices—and even the communities—in which the learning occurs. Occupational examples include learning to navigate (Hutchins 1983), weaving (Childs & Greenfield 1980), coal mining (Billett 1993a), dairy work (Scribner 1984), midwifery (Jordan 1989) and tailoring (Lave 1990).

Work practice can tacitly structure learners' access to the knowledge they need to acquire. Lave (1990) found that tailors' apprentices learnt by participating in work activities that inherently structured their engagement in increasingly more accountable tasks and gave them greater access to knowledge. This structuring is quite pedagogically sound. The apprentices move through experiences that first provide access to the global—the overall goals required for performance—then the local—the requirements for particular performance. The apprentices first finish and iron completed garments. This provides a basis for understanding the overall requirements for their work. Next they learn specific procedures for constructing garments. The pathway of learning experiences is 'formalised' by a progression of tasks that carry increasing levels of accountability—that is, movement from tasks of low to high accountability (i.e. those where mistakes can be tolerated to those where mistakes would have significant consequences). Both access to models for performance, and direct and indirect guidance, are provided for apprentices to learn tailoring on this pathway. In this way, the workplace experiences of the tailors' apprentices in terms of the activities they engage in are structured by their work practice (Lave 1990). In a similar way, Hutchins' (1983) study of fishermen learning to navigate demonstrates other aspects of deliberately structured approaches to learning. Substitute objects (shells and beach debris) were used to represent objects (star patterns) that cannot be seen during the day. Jordan (1989) demonstrates how Yucatan birth attendants learn their profession through the structured observation and imitation of more experienced practitioners. Their apprenticeship proceeds with little or no separation between daily life and the learning of the professional skills of midwifery. The Guarenos of the Orinoco Delta of Venezuela teach cultivation, animal husbandry, hunting and fishing in ways that are highly structured through learning by doing and being provided with an initial understanding of each task and its goals (Ruddle & Chesterfield 1978). These processes of learning vocational practices, which are essential to the communities in which they are practised, would be described by many as being 'informal'. Yet they are highly structured and formalised. Moreover, rather than being ad hoc or incidental, these kinds of experiences structure learning that can have transferable outcomes. Indeed, Rogoff (1982) and Rogoff and Gauvain (1984) found that the potential for transfer from this kind of learning was as great as that from school-based learning.

Nominated pathways of learning activities have also been identified in contemporary work settings. For instance, in hairdressing salons, the apprentices' tasks are determined by the particular salon's approach to hairdressing (Billett 1995a). For instance, in one salon where the client is serviced by a number of hairdressers, the apprentices learn first to keep the salon clean and tidy, and communicate with clients by asking whether and how they want tea or coffee. Through these activities, the apprentices learn about hygiene, cleanliness and procedures for determining client needs. More than 'busy work', these tasks are necessary components in understanding and initially participating in hairdressing practice. This initial participation includes the building of the apprentices' confidence to negotiate with clients. The apprentices may next learn how to wash clients' hair, and later rinse out the chemicals used to shape and colour hair. These tasks provide new skills and advance further what they have already learnt, such as communicating with clients in more intimate ways. Also, as they wash or rinse clients' hair, they learn about the important aspects of these tasks (e.g. the importance of removing all the chemicals) and their place and significance in the hairdressing process. The apprentices later work alongside experienced hairdressers, helping to place rods and curlers in clients' hair. Later still, before being permitted to cut and colour women's hair, they commence by cutting men's hair, which is seen as being less difficult and of lower accountability than cutting women's hair. This pathway of activities continues until the apprentices can style hair independently.

In another salon, however, where hairdressers have responsibility for the entire hairdressing task, the apprentice is required to learn to cut and colour far earlier than in the kind of salon referred to above. The structured pathway of activities in the second salon includes mastery of a set of procedures that permit independent practice early in the apprenticeship. So, in the same vocation, the particular goals and practices of the workplace will determine much of the structuring of learning.

Darrah (1996) has also shown how, in a computer manufacturing company, access to work is organised and sequenced to structure learning through a pathway of activities comprising the assembly and testing of computers. To take a further example, in commercial aviation there is a pathway of learning associated with movement from being a flight engineer, to first officer through to captain (Hutchins & Palen 1997).

There are organisational factors that clearly structure and distribute opportunities for workers to participate in workplaces. Seniority in workplaces (Dore & Sako 1989) and work demarcations (Danford 1998), as well as internal and external competition, restructuring and redeployment, all structure access to work tasks and hence to learning (Billett et al. 1997). Consequently, the bases for learning in workplaces are not ad hoc or without structure. They are formalised and structured by the goals, activities and culture of the work practice (Brown et al. 1989), just as learners' experiences in educational institutions are structured by those institutions' cultures of practice. As discussed in greater detail in subsequent chapters, workplaces are often highly contested, with access to the activities and guidance required for learning not being uniformly distributed. Opportunities to participate may be distributed on the basis of factors such as workplace cliques, affiliations, gender, race, language or employment standing and status. Indeed, it could be suggested that, rather than being unstructured, workplace learning experiences are structured by too many factors.

It is also misguided to make judgments about the quality of learning environments that are premised on the presence of qualified teachers. Teaching and rich learning are not necessarily synonymous. Instead of being passive and wholly dependent upon teachers, individuals actively and continually construct knowledge. Learning described as 'spectacular' occurs in children between their first and fifth years (Bransford et al. 1985, cited in Pea 1987). The language and social skills learnt during these years provide a basis for children to participate successfully in schooling. Yet this spectacular learning is not a product of direct teaching. Instead, it takes place through children's engagement in tasks, accessing indirect guidance and independent problem-solving. Rather than needing to be constantly taught by others, individuals are continuously and actively engaged in the process of learning. Having access to direct instruction provided by teachers is not a necessary condition for structured and focused learning to occur.

This is not to deny the important contributions that others can make to individuals' learning. Coworkers—particularly more experienced coworkers—play a significant role in learning. This role includes participation in shared (collaborative) problem-solving between the novice and more experienced worker. Collaborative problem-solving of this kind is viewed as being more important for individuals' construction of knowledge than the transmission of knowledge from one individual to another through direct teaching (Collins et al. 1989; Rogoff 1990, 1995; Resnick et al. 1997). The shared experiences of parent and child, tradesperson and novice, teacher and student are all examples of learning through collaborative activities. Such collaboration is invaluable by making accessible to learners what they might not be able to learn alone. This kind of close or direct guidance is often readily available in workplaces (Billett 1996b). Consequently, the quality of learning is not wholly premised on the presence of teachers as transmitters of knowledge. Instead, the kinds of activities engaged in by individuals and the support and guidance they can access in the workplace from other workers will influence the quality of learning at work. In this way, much of the knowledge required for demanding vocational practice can be learnt through work (Billett 1996b, 1998).

Learning through work

There is long-standing evidence of the efficacy of learning in the workplace. Prior to the establishment of vocational colleges and universities, most people learnt their vocations through their work. The evidence also suggests that workers have long produced goods and provided services with limited technology and in ways that have required understanding and robust (transferable) procedures developed through their work (e.g. Gimpel 1983; Keller & Keller 1993; Whalley & Barley 1997). The products and services of craft and other workers require combinations of creativity and functionality. Many of the world's great buildings, such as the castles, churches and cathedrals of Europe, were built by workers whose vocational practice was developed through participation in their craft (Gimpel 1983). Often, this knowledge was not committed to text, drawings or plans but learnt about and passed across generations of craft workers. Perhaps these were truly 'knowledge workers' who learnt their vocational knowledge through their work.

More recent examples of learning through workplace experiences in Japanese corporations also attest to their efficacy (Dore & Sako 1989; Lynch 1993). In these corporations, learning takes place on the job and is structured, with supervisors having the responsibility for developing the work-related knowledge of their subordinates. Much of what apprentices learn during their three- or four-year indenture is also a product of engagement in everyday work practice. This learning often generates capabilities that are transferable across tasks and situations. Learning in the workplace cannot, therefore, be described as concrete—fixed and embedded inextricably in the circumstances of its acquisition. Instead, at least some of what is been learnt in workplaces is transferable to other situations.

Conversely, it is reasonable to question assumptions about the transferability of learning in educational institutions. Even in specifically focused vocational education courses, students often experience frustration and disillusionment when attempting to apply what they have learnt to workplace tasks (Raizen 1994). Much of this transfer problem can be associated with the different ways that the knowledge learnt is contextualised in schools and workplaces. I recall my halting attempts to apply college-learnt knowledge to my first job in the clothing industry. The tasks were different to those I had been prepared for and had learnt about at college. The procedures used in the factory were unknown to me and the context in which the work was being conducted was quite remote from my previous (college-based) experience. It was not a case of others telling me to forget what I had learnt in college. It was more that my learning was not applicable to or intelligible in the workplace. While many of the concepts and procedures learnt at college were useful, they were manifested in ways that either masked or were different from those experienced at college. It was only years later, when I had experienced a number of different clothing manufacturing workplaces and practices, that the commonalities to the approaches to work tasks became apparent. So how robust was my college-learnt knowledge? It is important, as Rogoff (1982, 1984) warns, not to assume that knowledge learnt in either workplaces or educational institutions will be either wholly situational specific or wholly transferable.

It is imprecise to refer to workplaces as 'informal' learning settings. Workplace experiences are likely to be structured by the enterprise's work practices (i.e. its goals and procedures), just as students' experiences in educational institutions are. The key difference lies in what is 'formalised'. Also, teaching and rich learning are not always synonymous, as transferable learning can occur without the presence of teachers. The absence of teachers does not of itself condemn learning outcomes to be weak and concrete. Learning can be independent and interdependent, with the latter probably best able to be achieved through guidance rather than direct teaching. It is also inaccurate to characterise workplace learning as concrete. Learning in any environment will be more or less transferable, depending on the quality of learning processes experienced. Therefore, the same claims about the structure, adaptability and robustness of outcomes can be made of workplaces as of educational institutions. With this in mind, the next section presents an overview of how individuals learn in the workplace from a constructivist perspective by describing the processes by which the construction of knowledge takes place.

LEARNING AND WORK: ACTIVITIES AND GUIDANCE

Learning and working are interdependent. We learn constantly through engaging in conscious goal-directed everyday activities—indeed, as we think and act, we learn. However, the quality of this learning is likely to depend on: (a) the kinds of activities that individuals engage in; (b) their access to the contribution of situational factors, including support and guidance; and (c) how individuals engage, interact and interpretatively construct knowledge from these situations. Together, these factors influence the process of learning and what is learnt. In doing so, they reflect the interdependence between work and learning, providing a basis to consider not only the contributions of the workplace as a learning environment, but also how the workplace might be organised to improve learning.

Central to understanding learning in the workplace are the tasks or activities in which individuals engage at work. These activities are variously familiar (routine) or new (non-routine). The term 'routine' is used to avoid the difficulty of describing activities that are more or less demanding of learners, because such demands are usually person dependent. Tasks that can be viewed as routine within a workplace are those that occur commonly. Both kinds of activities require individuals to engage in thinking and acting processes from which they construct and/or reinforce and organise their knowledge (Ericsson & Simon 1984). Engagement in workplace activities is more than just completing work tasks; it results in learning of different kinds, as illustrated by the vignette at the beginning of this chapter. In order to understand learning through everyday activities in the workplace, the consequences of engaging in these kinds of activities need to be discussed.

Engagement in routine tasks

Common or routine work tasks are a key source of learning about vocational practice. Engaging in routine or familiar tasks in the workplace reinforces what we already know. This kind of learning is essential for performance at work, because it strengthens the knowledge we use in responding to these tasks. Even when undertaking highly routine tasks such as changing gears in a car, typing on a keyboard or chopping vegetables, we are reinforcing what we know and do. During these kinds of activities, we monitor our performance against the intended goal (smooth gear changes, correct letters typed, fine dice of onion) in order to sustain or improve our performance. In doing so, we strengthen our performance through minor adjustments and adaptations. Outcomes associated with this reinforcement are improvements in performance and the satisfaction derived from achieving the desired goal: securing viability (von Glasersfeld 1987). By repeating an activity and achieving the goal (e.g. success in changing gears), we have engaged our existing knowledge and reinforced our way of successfully completing this activity.

This process of learning has been described as undertaking increasingly mature approximations of the task (Brown & Palinscar

1989; Collins et al. 1989). This means that, as individuals practise the task, they monitor their performance and gradually improve on the task that has been modelled to them and from which they create conceptual models. Eventually, they are able to perform the task to the standard of the modelled performance. It is through such a process that the concepts associated with the activity (e.g. how to change gears) are progressively transformed into single, smooth procedures through a process referred to as *compilation* (Anderson 1982).

Once this has taken place, conscious thinking is no longer required to perform routine tasks—which is why such routine tasks as changing gears, hammering nails or rolling curlers into clients' hair can be undertaken almost subconsciously. However, although these activities are performed seemingly automatically, monitoring and refinements occur constantly. This explains why car owners are usually unable to discern that their brakes are wearing down, or their clutch is gaining more travel. Fine adjustments have been made (e.g. a firmer foot on the brake and a longer compression of the clutch) tacitly to compensate for brake and clutch wear. These adjustments are monitored and executed by higher orders of procedures (Evans 1991a; Stevenson 1991) that act on compiled knowledge to manage their deployment and secure further refinements.

Compilation comprises two learning processes: proceduralisation and composition (Anderson 1982; Glaser 1990). *Proceduralisation* is the movement from procedures having to be consciously thought about to their becoming 'automated'. Moreover, through repeated practice, separate parts of the task are transformed into a single procedure, rather than needing to be thought about and consciously executed as a set of separate procedures. Consequently, instead of having to consciously think about the separate stages of changing gears, this task is transformed into a single smooth procedure (or production) that requires little conscious thinking. This learning process is referred to as *composition*, defined as the collapsing of a series of procedures into a single procedure (Anderson 1982). Similar processes occur with associations between concepts. Frequent associations lead to strengthened links between concepts (e.g. red = stop; green = go; or a consistent problem with a particular machine or product). Through repeated associations, these links are strengthened until the use of one readily prompts the other. This strengthening permits the almost instantaneous categorisation of and response to tasks by experts (Pea 1993). These associations become *chunked*, in a process much like composition, again easing the need for conscious thought. Consequently, upon seeing a red traffic light, we engage in a process of slowing down and changing down through the gears, without recourse to conscious thought. Equally, when encountering the particular machine or product that we associate with past problems, we are automatically primed to be cautious. As with compilation, the chunking of concepts about work practice enables us to concentrate on other aspects of the tasks we are undertaking, because parts of the task can be performed seemingly automatically. Through everyday practice, it has become easy to conduct these tasks; we are able to undertake the activity with little demand being placed on conscious thought.

These kinds of learning are therefore necessary for performance at work. We would achieve little if every element of a work task required conscious thought and monitoring. While human memories are powerful, it seems our minds are not particularly good at processing lots of knowledge simultaneously (Newell & Simon 1972). Our conscious thinking processes can only manage a limited number of items at once—perhaps no more than seven (Miller 1956). The processes of compiling and composing procedures and chunking concepts required to perform routine work tasks ease the demands on conscious memory. This permits us to use conscious thinking processes to engage in and monitor other activities simultaneously. For instance, because experienced electricians have compiled and chunked their knowledge of wiring power points, they can think about other tasks while they wire a power point. They are able to strip away the outer coating of the cable effortlessly, unscrew fittings and quickly recognise which wire has to be fastened to which component as effortlessly as experienced drivers negotiate the familiar journey to work. However, novice electricians, who have not yet compiled and chunked these skills and associations, have to consciously focus on each part of the task until practice renders them automatic, thereby requiring less conscious attention. Therefore, when undertaking a new task, it is necessary to attend consciously to each part of the task. Novices cannot simultaneously engage in planning other tasks and the strategic monitoring of the tasks they are currently performing. Imagine how difficult it would be to walk if every movement of the legs and their coordination had to be consciously thought about. Instead, after practice, these routine tasks become procedures we can use whilst undertaking other tasks. This is because the compilation of procedures and the chunking of concepts frees up our conscious thinking to focus on other activities. Without such processes, we would be overwhelmed by the demands of conscious thought in undertaking routine activities.

Routine workplace tasks provide the opportunities required for repeated performance that lead to the compilation of procedures and forming associations among concepts. Unfortunately, opportunities to engage in routine tasks are rarely available in educational institutions, except where those activities relate to the routine activities particular to these institutions. In teaching students in vocational colleges, exercise tasks are usually repeated once or twice before moving on to the next task. Students may be denied opportunities to compile procedures and chunk concepts in these circumstances. In educational institutions, students are often engaged in mainly non-routine activities without opportunities to practise and reinforce. As a junior designer in the garment manufacturing industry, I was required to work on the production line in order to understand how the garments were manufactured. This entailed spending days at each workstation until I was able to perform tasks to the required standards of quality and speed. Only then was I permitted to proceed to the next workstation. Now, many years later, I could still probably perform many of those tasks—and, with some practice, to the required standard. Opportunities to practise and reinforce need to be seen as necessary parts of learning any work task. Routine workplace activities provide these opportunities.

However, it is important to acknowledge another side to the compilation of procedures and chunking of concepts. When circumstances change or a reappraisal of approaches is required, automated knowledge may resist change. For example, when you travel to another country and have to drive on the opposite side of the road from the one you are used to, your automated knowledge does not always easily adapt. Indeed, it might even work against you, particularly if you are engaged in a number of activities simultaneously. Because the gearshift and indicators are not where you expect, you have to do more than think about driving on the 'other side' of the road. When dealing with one task at a time, we can manage these kinds of demands without conscious thought. However, when turning right off one street, you may find yourself on the 'wrong side' of another with windscreen wipers operating instead of indicators and the car almost stalling as you attempt to locate the correct gear with a hand not used to this task. This confusion arises because we cannot simultaneously and consciously process wholesale changes or so much new knowledge. In the same way, changes in work activities can also cause confusion when our well-practised procedures no longer apply. Here, the automated procedures and chunked concepts need to be modified to the new situations. Conscious thought is required to monitor and make the appropriate changes. In other words, new knowledge has to be constructed in response to, and as a product of, addressing these new work requirements.

New knowledge: Engaging in non-routine activities

We construct new knowledge through engaging in activities that are new or novel to us. This is because, in undertaking these kinds of activities, the necessary problem-solving transforms and extends our existing knowledge. Not all activities in workplaces are routine. Tasks have to be undertaken that workers have not encountered before, and these tasks might be novel—either in whole or in part. The analogy of a journey can be used to illustrate this process. For instance, say you want to travel to an unfamiliar part of town. You have to think about how to get there (plan and establish goals) and speculate on what might be there when you arrive. When you actually engage in this goal-directed activity, you are faced with options, impasses and unforeseen circumstances that you have to deal with (what lane to be in, where to turn and where the intersections are). At the end of the journey, as well as reaching the destination, you will have learnt new things about the route. You can now also make judgments about the journey and destination. Your existing knowledge has been extended and transformed (you know how to get there), new associations are established (this street intersects with one that you already knew about) and your ability to realise the task is confirmed. The learning outcomes include the development of the procedures to get there and the route taken, and concepts associated with the journey and destination. However, this learning process is underpinned by how individuals value the journey and destination. If an individual does not actively engage in the learning process, their learning outcomes might be quite weak. Referred to as *dispositions* (Perkins et al. 1993), the individual's attitude to the journey and destination (i.e. value placed on it, interest in it) influences how the task is conceptualised and how knowledge about the task is organised. For instance, was it a frustrating drive and the destination not worth the effort or was the trip worthwhile? The circumstances of the learning and the learner's interpretation of that experience result in an individual's categorisation of the learning of new knowledge. Throughout the journey, the engagement in goal-directed activity (problem-solving) extends and transforms the individual's existing knowledge.

Although the example here is of a car journey, the same goes for any vocational activity. The scenario presented at the beginning of the chapter represents such an example. Equally, hairdressers, when asked to perform techniques that are unfamiliar, or to work with new clients, are extending the breadth and organisation of their knowledge about hairdressing and the procedures required in their jobs. As these techniques are practised, the new procedures improve or evolve, possibly influencing future work. In this way, through undertaking non-routine work tasks, individuals construct new knowledge.

When attempting to do something new, we use our existing knowledge and tools of different kinds to close the gap between what we already know and what we need to know. Routine tasks are usually well defined. However, responding to new or non-routine tasks requires conscious thought and is directly associated with new learning. With new tasks, it is unlikely that all variables will be known. So individuals may draw upon additional resources to understand the task more fully and attempt to close the gap between what they know and what they need to know. For instance, they might recall similar situations from their past to establish a basis for proceeding with the task. Alternatively, they may use tools of different kinds when engaged in these activities. In the journey example, a map to which we apply our existing knowledge of streets and districts might aid the journey to an unfamiliar part of town. To close the gap in our knowledge, we use the map to work through the task (identifying roads, places to turn, etc.). In workplaces, instead of maps, there may be models, clues and cues for how to proceed, such as access to previously completed jobs or even half-completed jobs (Lave 1990) or the layout of the workplace (Billett 1994a). In these ways, the tools and artefacts of the workplace aid the learning of new knowledge.

However, some work tasks will be too novel or difficult to be resolved satisfactorily. For example, if you do not understand the principles of a new piece of equipment or are faced with a work problem that is totally different from anything you have experienced before, it would be unreasonable to expect task resolution. This is a *transfer* problem. When we are able to transfer our knowledge to a work situation easily—for example, learning to use a piece of equipment or a procedure similar to one we have already mastered—this is referred to as *near transfer* (Royer 1979). The transfer of knowledge to a new situation is referred to as *far transfer*. For instance, transferring from a manually-operated to a computer-operated lathe is likely to be far transfer, because their operation is quite different (Martin & Scribner 1991). However, sometimes the transfer task is simply too difficult—it is 'too far'. Novices face this situation far more frequently than experts, because they are more likely to confront novel workplace tasks. In these situations, workers may be unable to find ways of using existing knowledge to transform and resolve the problem. Knowledge of European cuisine may not be sufficient to permit an experienced chef to prepare authentic Southeast Asian food. These are the situations where the contributions of more experienced coworkers are most useful in guiding the learning of knowledge (procedures and concepts) that cannot be learnt alone.

Nonetheless, learning occurs even in situations where transfer is 'too far'. Having failed to produce a dish satisfactorily, the chef might be motivated to learn something more about this cuisine. Alternatively, failure to produce the dish satisfactorily might result in a rejection of this cuisine by the chef. There are also tasks which are undertaken infrequently (e.g. annual tax returns) that require conscious attempts to reconstruct what we have partially learnt previously. From these examples, it can be seen that making the 'far' transfer nearer is an important goal in assisting individuals to learn new knowledge. Workplace artefacts, the workplace itself, experienced others and peers can all assist in bridging the gap between what the individual knows and what may otherwise remain unknowable. In the case of the tax returns, we might use the previous year's return as an artefact and tool to guide the filling out of this year's return.

In the above discussion, learning through everyday activity has been characterised as being either routine or non-routine (see Figure 1.1). The ability to engage in non-routine as well as routine activity is also a key determinant of how learning in the workplace can assist in extending learners' knowledge. However, there are degrees of routineness that sit between the two extremes. The processes of compilation and chunking described earlier take the task from being novel through to being routine. They exemplify learning that moves across this continuum as it progresses from being non-routine to routine practice. Many of the activities we engage in during our everyday experience in the workplace have combinations of routineness. These make different kinds of demands on learners and require different kinds of guidance—and, of course, they result in different kinds of learning.

CONCEPTUAL BASES OF WORKPLACE LEARNING

The ideas proposed above are well supported by the literature on learning and development, particularly within constructivist theories. These theories propose that humans are active in making sense of their world—that is, learning. Their construction of knowledge is premised on what they already know and have experienced. According to this view, humans are not empty vessels waiting to be filled with

Figure 1.1 Learning through everyday activity

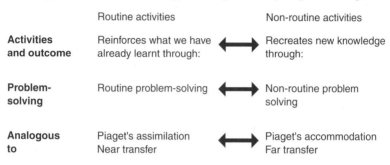

	Routine activities		Non-routine activities
Activities and outcome	Reinforces what we have already learnt through:	⟷	Recreates new knowledge through:
Problem-solving	Routine problem-solving	⟷	Non-routine problem solving
Analogous to	Piaget's assimilation Near transfer	⟷	Piaget's accommodation Far transfer

knowledge or sponges waiting to absorb external sources of knowledge, as behavioural theory proposes (Bijou 1990). Instead, humans actively strive to make sense of the world. Therefore, from the constructivist perspective, learning is ongoing and unavoidable as we think and act. It seems that we can no more consciously avoid learning than we can breathing. Constructivist theorists, including Piaget (1966), Vygotsky (1978), von Glasersfeld (1987) and Rogoff (1990, 1995), propose that individuals construct knowledge interpretatively from what they experience in the 'lived' world—including, of course, workplaces. Piaget (1966) refers to individuals maintaining equilibrium in their encounters with everyday tasks and activities. We seek to make sense of the world and attempt to overcome confusion in what we experience: disequilibrium. Therefore, equilibrium is a goal that requires the integration of new information with what individuals already know—seeking the viability of what they experience, as von Glasersfeld (1987) proposes. The analogy here is one of balance: individuals strive to maintain balance when faced with changes that attempt to throw them off balance. Therefore, in seeking equilibrium, there is an attempt to balance what the individual already knows with what they experience. The process of securing equilibrium or viability is clearly not restricted to experiences in classrooms, nor to the attention of teachers. Equilibrium is ongoing in all aspects of thinking and acting. In this way, everyday work experiences provide opportunities for individuals to learn. However, that learning is premised on their existing knowledge and interests.

Piaget (1966) maintains that humans are driven towards maintaining their equilibrium through the processes of assimilation and accommodation. *Assimilation* involves using existing knowledge in order to respond to a particular task or stimulus, incorporating the new experience into that existing knowledge (Piaget 1966). When responding to stimuli such as sound or shapes, we listen or observe using our existing knowledge to understand or interpret those things that we already know about—for instance, evaluating new software in terms of how previous software worked. *Accommodation*, on the other hand, is the process of developing new knowledge (categories or subsystems) when faced with a new situation. The established knowledge structures or behaviours remain, but are differentiated by the introduction of a new subsystem (Piaget 1976). So, when faced with new software, understanding the novel features of the software leads to a transformation of our knowledge. We have augmented our understanding through accommodating its new features. Of course, accommodation is far more demanding than assimilation. It requires effort, so an interest in extending knowledge is likely to be required. Everyday workplace activities provide opportunities for engagement in both assimilation and accommodation (Billett 1996a) through participation in routine and non-routine work tasks. As noted earlier, these tasks assist the construction and reinforcement of the knowledge required for work tasks and, in so doing, structure the organisation of that knowledge.

The cognitive literature asserts quite directly that learning is through problem-solving (e.g. Rogoff 1990; Shuell 1990; Anderson 1993). For instance, Rogoff (1990: 8) holds that 'cognition and thinking are defined as problem-solving, with thinking being functional and grounded in goal-directed activity'. Everyday work tasks demonstrate participation in goal-directed activities. Also, Van Lehn (1988: 38) claims that learning results from resolving a problem, with 'learning only occurring when an impasse occurs'. However, more than just adding to knowledge, new learning influences the organisation of individuals' knowledge, including making connections and interacting with prior knowledge (Prawat 1989). Accordingly, individuals' existing knowledge and cognitive processes work together to further develop knowledge when they are engaged in everyday goal-directed activity at work. The cognitive literature also explicitly proposes problem-solving as being of the two kinds referred to earlier: routine and non-routine (Groen & Patel 1988; Prawat 1989). Through our engagement in everyday goal-directed work activities, we learn through what Rogoff (1995) refers to as 'moment-by-moment' learning or microgenetic development. Similarly, Lave (1993: 5), an anthropologist, concluded from a series of studies of work that '[it is difficult to avoid] the conclusion that learning is ubiquitous in on-going activity, though often unrecognised as such'. So the basis for learning through everyday activity is well founded in these theoretical traditions.

The interdependence which exists between learning and work is founded, on the one hand, in what the workplace provides to assist that learning and, on the other, in how the individual engages and uses these contributions. These are themes that recur throughout this book. In order to preview these themes, the next two sections identify the contributions to learning provided by the workplace. Then—as individuals ultimately determine what they learn as a consequence of their engagement in work—they outline the basis for individuals' construction of knowledge.

WORKPLACE CONTRIBUTIONS TO LEARNING

The context in which thinking, acting and learning take place is rarely neutral (Brown et al. 1989; Greeno 1997). And the prospect of structured and transferable learning is not necessarily premised on whether the learning occurs as part of a program in educational institutions. Instead, the kinds of activities learners engage in, and the quality of support and guidance they receive, are significant in determining whether rich learning results. Situational factors such as those found in workplaces influence individuals' learning in three ways. First, the particular situation provides the kinds of activities in which individuals engage, the problems to be solved, the knowledge to be constructed and the goals for their successful resolution. Second, the direct guidance available in the workplace provides the basis for collaborative learning between the learner and more experienced workers. Third, the workplace provides indirect guidance in the form of opportunities to observe other workers, contributions of the physical workplace setting and its tools. These contributions to learning in workplaces are discussed in detail in Chapter 3, however they are introduced and discussed briefly below.

Activities in which individuals engage

The kinds of activities in which individuals engage in workplaces will influence what and how they will learn and how they organise what they have learnt (Rogoff & Lave 1984). Particular kinds of workplace tasks are likely to result in particular kinds of learning because of the kinds of problem-solving they present. For instance, learning about coal mining through classroom activities or through activities in a coal mine will engage learners in quite different kinds of problem-solving activities. Consequently, different learning outcomes will result. Consider the different kinds of 'moment-by-moment' learning (Rogoff 1995) that would occur in each circumstance because of the differences in the knowledge-constructing and reinforcing tasks that each situation presents to learners. For instance, moment-by-moment learning in the coal mine will arise from everyday tasks such as the use of equipment, grading of product and monitoring of production. In the classroom, moment-by-moment learning will arise as a result of engagement in instructional activities shaped by those practices. Differences in these activities influence the prospect of transfer of knowledge across situations, which helps to explain limits on the transferability of learning in classroom-type activities to non-classroom-like activities. Neither situation presents a neutral basis for learning—they each structure learning in particular ways. Furthermore, learning about coal mining in an open cut or an underground coal mine will lead to quite different outcomes, due to the variations in techniques, divisions of labour, work habits and traditions deployed in each type of mining. The knowledge-constructing tasks and direct guidance are quite different in the work practices of these two kinds of coal mining.

When first teaching in a technical college, I recall having a strong sense that the activities my students were engaged in were quite different from what happened in actual clothing manufacture. Because of resource limitations in the college, I had to develop substitute techniques to teach students. Consequently, the students were not engaged in authentic practices of pattern-making that would readily be recognisable in clothing manufacturing workplaces. They were learning substitute tasks that were constrained by the resources and activities of the educational institution. The important point here is that workplace activities are authentic in terms of actual vocational practice. The kind of learning arising from authentic activities overcomes the first transfer task for much learning—that from the classroom to the workplace. The opportunity to learn new vocational knowledge and then reinforce it through practice in the workplace is a firm foundation for developing transferable vocational knowledge.

However, although authentic in terms of actual practice, there can be no guarantee that the activities in one workplace will be compatible with activities in another, even when the same vocational practice is occurring. For instance, as already discussed, different hairdressing salons have different performance goals and practices (Billett 1995a). Therefore, all aspects of vocational practice learnt in one workplace cannot be guaranteed to transfer effectively to another. So, while the authenticity of workplace learning activities is a real strength in terms of its application to particular work practice, there will still be limits in the transferability of this knowledge to other work situations that differ from those in which the knowledge was learnt.

Direct guidance by others

Guidance from other workers assists the development of vocational practice. More experienced workers contribute to learning vocational practice by assisting the learning of procedures and ideas that are difficult and unlikely to be learnt by discovery alone. These kinds of learning can best be achieved through joint problem-solving between the learner and a more experienced social partner who provides access to knowledge (Vygotsky 1978). Guidance and collaborative problem-solving with coworkers can make this knowledge accessible and therefore able to be learnt by workers. The kind of learning required for independent performance at work will likely result from collaborative thinking and acting between the expert and novice, rather than through the transmission of knowledge where learners remain passive recipients of the knowledge to be learnt. Vygotsky (1978) referred to this joint problem-solving as *proximal* (close) *guidance* and to the collaborative learning process as the Zone of Proximal Development (ZPD)—the enhanced scope of learning likely to result from close guidance provided by a more experienced worker. An important quality of close guidance in the workplace is the access it provides to components of vocational procedures and concepts that learners are unlikely to discover alone (Billett 1996a). These are often referred to as 'tricks of the trade'. In short, the quality of direct interaction accessible in a workplace is a key determinant in the quality of learning outcomes. This extends to the availability of this guidance, the willingness of individuals to assist others and the skill experienced coworkers have in sharing this knowledge. Many of these ideas and principles are consistent with adult learning theory, which emphasises the facilitation of learners and their self-directed learning rather than didactic teaching (Knowles 1984; Tennant 1997).

Indirect guidance in the workplace

Indirect kinds of guidance also contribute to learning in workplaces. These contributions are found in the social and physical environment of the workplace. They include interactions with other workers, observing and listening to other workers, objects and artefacts (Hutchins 1993; Resnick et al. 1997). The contributions of the physical environment to thinking and acting are often overlooked. But consider how difficult the weekly task of grocery shopping would be without the aisles arranged in ways that permit you to find particular kinds of grocery items and then identify products by their shape, labelling and colour. Instead, imagine if you had to conduct your shopping by identifying what you wanted from a set of similarly shaped and coloured labels displayed in no particular order. The physical environment of the workplace provides tools, clues and cues that assist our thinking. In addition, the engagement with artefacts and physical tools in the workplace is likely to be necessary for performance. There are strong relationships between an individual's tools and their performance (Wertsch 1998). Without the lathe, the machinist cannot know how to turn the piece of metal. Without the sewing machine, the tailor cannot make garments and understand fully how these garments have to be sewn.

As noted earlier, tailors' apprentices were guided indirectly through the observation of other workers, their access to half-completed garments and the sequencing of activities (Lave 1990). Observing other workers provides goals for activities and/or sub-goals for stages or components of tasks. It also provides a basis for learners to compare their performance with that of others. The physical setting contributes clues and cues for both tasks and performance within those tasks. Lave (1990) has shown how partly constructed garments provided apprentices with a means of proceeding with making their own. To take another example, a warehouse worker referred to the variations of packed pallets available in a warehouse as a library of options that were accessible when a novel pallet-packing task had to be undertaken (Billett 1993b). In these ways, the workplace provides learners with an environment from which to access important contributions to learning that are indirect yet inherent and ongoing in the workplace.

In sum, workplaces determine the sorts of learning tasks that individuals engage in, the kinds of goals required and the guidance individuals can access. Rather than being neutral, the circumstances in which activities—and hence learning—occur, constitute active components in the learning process (Brown et al. 1989). Such is the complexity of these factors and their contributions to learning that to describe them as incidental or informal is both misleading and imprecise. They are structured and central to doing, knowing and learning.

INDIVIDUAL INFLUENCES ON LEARNING

Although pervasive, the contributions of situational factors do not wholly determine how and what individuals learn. Learning is not a process of socialisation determined by the situation (e.g. work-place) in which the individual is engaged in thinking and acting. Individuals in the workplace still determine how and what they learn. They ultimately construct knowledge and determine what they appropriate, what they ignore and what they merely learn in a superficial way (Wertsch 1998). How individuals engage in work-place activities and the learning that results from those activities is unlikely to be uniform. This is because each individual uses different bases for thinking and acting at work. Rather than simply 'internalising' knowledge through these experiences, each indivi-dual's learning is influenced by the knowledge that they possess and bring to the situation. These individual influences are the product of personal histories. The actual process of learning—of making sense of things—is a reciprocal process through which the learner also transforms their view of the source of knowledge (Valsiner 1994). This simply means that learning is not a one-way process. Through considering the quality of the advice received, we form or revise judgments about the source of the knowledge. For instance, when discussing a problem with experts in the workplace, we make judgments about the knowledge that is being provided and the credibility of its source. From these encounters, we might appreciate further the qualities of the expert. Alternatively, we might decide that the expert is particularly knowledgeable about certain matters, but not others. When we try to apply the advice, we make further judgments about the quality of the information. Accordingly, how we view the expert is transformed: their standing might be enhanced or diminished, or it might be refined further. The same goes for a book or film. We might have heard about the qualities of the book or film; however, upon seeing the film or reading the book, we might agree or disagree with the reputation that preceded it. Regardless, our view of the book/film will be trans-formed, because we have learnt more about it. A reciprocal process is associated with this learning, through which both the source (the experience) and the subject (the learner) are transformed. It is not merely an imitative or reproductive response.

Learning new knowledge takes effort. This is particularly so for adults, for whom new knowledge requires a reappraisal and reorganisation of what they know and the structuring of their knowledge—as in the process of accommodation. Constructing new categories of learning, reformulating understandings and developing new procedures are all highly demanding. Because routine problem-solving is less demanding than non-routine problem-solving, adult learners might prefer to tackle the task using existing knowledge (assimilation) rather than engage in more demanding thinking and acting (accommodation). Adults tend to organise knowledge on the basis of its usefulness in previous circumstances. So—perhaps understandably—adult learners may want to assimilate rather than accommodate, because the former is less demanding and challenging, and has previously provided certainty.

Therefore, in addition to the workplace's contributions, individuals' interpretative construction of knowledge is a key determinant of the quality of workplace learning. Depending on what they have learnt and experienced during their lives, adults will engage selectively according to the kinds of learning they believe are desirable and the effort they decide to expend. This influences what they learn and how they organise their knowledge, as well as attitudes associated with learning new knowledge. Consequently, individuals are unlikely to construct knowledge uniformly or without reflection on their beliefs and procedures. For example, workers exposed to unethical activity or unsafe working practices are likely to make judgments about those activities. Some might accept these practices unquestioningly, or do so because they want to gain acceptance within a work group. Others may refuse to accept certain situations, even when those situations are accepted as useful practice. Workers' values also have powerful influences on how they approach work. For instance, underground coal miners may view learning about open cut mining as beneath their dignity, as this kind of mining is the work of 'rock apes'. Hence their values and beliefs may be antagonised by this task and they are unlikely to engage enthusiastically in learning this work. Although these miners have rich coal mining knowledge, it is of a particular kind—one that privileges underground mining over open cut mining operations. Alternatively, another individual with heavy earthmoving experience may view this opportunity quite differently. Darrah (1996) illustrates the consequences of clashes between workers' cultural norms and the practice within an American computer manufacturing company. Workers of Vietnamese heritage rejected teamwork because being appraised as a team member rather than as individuals clashed with their cultural norms. Consequently, these workers resisted participation in and learning about teamwork. It is important to be aware that workplace learning is not simply imitative, merely reproducing what is encountered. It can be interpretivist and reflective, and even critical, as is proposed in Chapter 4.

SUMMARY

Learning and working are interdependent. Work practices provide and structure activities and guidance in ways that influence the learning of the knowledge required for performance at work. These experiences are not informal or unstructured, as is often contended; instead, they are structured by the requirements of work practice rather than the practice of educational institutions. The types of activities individuals engage in and the guidance they access are central to learning the knowledge required for work. Workplace experiences are often of a kind that is unlikely to be replicated in educational institutions or through substitute means. The knowledge constructed in workplaces is likely to be different from that constructed in the classroom, rather than being inherently inferior. This is because the activities individuals engage in, and the kinds of guidance and support that contribute to learning, are different. Each of these settings has goals and activities that are the product of their institutional practices. In particular, workplace learning experiences are likely to be authentic in terms of the goal-directed activity of the workplace. To reiterate, the contributions of the workplace to learning are rich, complex and probably difficult to avoid. They are certainly neither incidental nor ad hoc. They are central to the workplace itself. The key concern is for these contributions to be directed towards developing transferable vocational knowledge that is purposeful for the individual and the enterprise in which they are employed.

So individuals learn as part of everyday work activity. But to what degree is the learning transferable or robust? What evidence is there that the outcome of learning is not of limited worth—concrete, ad hoc and incidental? How can workplace learning assist individuals to develop transferable knowledge that will address their development and their ability to perform in a particular workplace? These questions are the focus of subsequent chapters. In particular, the next chapter examines the kinds of knowledge required for workplace performance, as a basis for understanding the goals for evaluating learning arrangements for the workplace.

2

Expertise at work

The large bulldozer had slipped over the edge of the coal wall when the ground beneath it subsided. It lay precariously on an angle, about a third of the way down the side of the open cut coal mine. If it slipped further, it would probably roll and be wrecked on impact at the bottom. It was decided that the best way to retrieve the bulldozer was to shift a drag-line (a huge excavator with a bucket the size of a house) to pull it up the side of the open cut mine. This would be expensive, as it meant stopping the productive use of the drag-line and shifting it, including its power cables and transformers—a process that would take some days to complete. However, one worker decided to try another option. He went down to the bulldozer. After some work, he was able to get the oil and hydraulic pressures to operating levels. Then he slowly and carefully began to use the bulldozer to carve a temporary track up the side of the coal pit. It took time and care. But the bulldozer was retrieved unharmed and there was no need to stop production, nor to shift the drag-line. The worker who achieved this feat already had a reputation for being good at his job. However, his capacity to resolve this difficult situation cemented his standing in the workplace as an expert.

The client returned to the hairdressing salon in tears. Although she had been pleased with her new haircut when she left the salon, her husband had described it as making her look like a 'bikie's moll'. Peter, the hairdresser, gave her lots of sympathy, attention and a cup of coffee and showed concern about her plight. He gave her a particularly long shampoo and head massage, partly to relax her and partly to gain time to consider possible options. He discussed these options with the client, and they decided to tint her hair back to its natural colour, which would remove the bleached hair her husband disliked, then reshape the existing quite short cut. This would result in the client receiving a shorter, but similar, cut to the one she had had before. Peter also discreetly asked the apprentice to quickly contact the next couple of clients and reschedule their appointments until later in the day. During the next hour or so, Peter worked on the client's hair. He was jolly and chatted; he had her laughing and talking about the conservativeness of her husband. Eventually, when the treatment was finished, he led the client to the door, refusing her repeated offers to pay more. As she left, he sighed briefly then turned to apologise to the next client, who by now had been waiting for some time. Again, he took particular care to lavish attention on her, and confided in her some of the reasons why the appointment had been delayed.

The technician was the third person to attempt to sort out the problem. The apparently routine task of installing upgraded software was not working. Each time it was installed, at the last moment the system declined to accept the new program and the machine froze. She worked through the cycle once and then, having experienced the lockup herself, checked the system thoroughly. All the settings seemed correct. Next she asked the user about the history of the computer. This revealed that there had been an upgrade of memory recently, using sets of 16 units of RAM. The kind of memory was compatible with the machine, but this upgrade identified an area of difference between this machine and others in the workplace. It also reminded her of a problem she had experienced previously with this kind of computer. Borrowing units of memory from another computer and installing them, both the technician and the operator were pleased to see that the system immediately accepted the new software program. The fault and its source had been identified. Later, the technician explained the source of the problem to her coworkers. One of the technicians who had failed to resolve the problem admitted he would never have considered the problem to reside in incompatible memory, nor would he have thought of using the methods that she had used.

Individuals who are effective at work, who can handle difficult tasks such as those illustrated above, possess particular attributes. Technically, it is referred to as expertise. These are the individuals from whom others seek advice about how to approach a difficult task. Their attributes set them apart from less experienced workers and are also the qualities that other workers aspire to and employers wish more of their employees possessed. These attributes represent the kind of outcomes that should be developed through workplace learning. In order to assist the development of expertise, we need to understand the attributes that constitute expert performance at work. This enables the identification of the goals for workplace learning and selecting particular strategies to most effectively generate expertise in workers. Understanding these attributes can also help establish bases for guiding the development of and judgments about the effectiveness of workplace learning arrangements.

These attributes comprise the ability to respond effectively to both the everyday (routine) and new (non-routine) work tasks encountered in the workplace. Being effective with everyday workplace tasks is essential, but it is not sufficient for expert performance at work. It is also important and necessary to respond to new and unanticipated tasks. For individual workers, the ability to transfer their vocational knowledge within the enterprise as new tasks arise and to other work situations is an important attribute— one that opens up options and opportunities for their vocational advancement (e.g. promotion, portability). Workers' ability to accomplish new tasks as well as the everyday ones enhances the prospect of the enterprise being able to respond successfully to new work challenges (new work tasks) and changing environments (different ways of undertaking that work). Such responses require workers to have expert attributes. Therefore it is important to understand these attributes and how they can best be developed in the workplace.

UNDERSTANDING PERFORMANCE AT WORK

The requirements for performance at work vary within and across different vocations. Even when the same vocation is being practised, the requirements for work can be quite specific to a particular workplace. These requirements are also constantly changing as the technology, goals, tasks and personnel that comprise the work practice change. Also, the tendency to underestimate the complexity of vocational practice—particularly that not labelled as professional, technical or trade—has resulted in assumptions about some work which need to be challenged. Therefore, the requirements for expert vocational practice need to be identified in terms of their particular (i.e. specific workplace) and general (i.e. vocational practice) applications, as well as their changing nature.

The diverse requirements of work

Work practices are unlikely ever to be uniform. They differ across countries and within industries. Bailey (1993) has noted how the labour-intensive bundle system still dominates garment manufacturing in Japan, whereas highly automated manufacturing procedures and robotics are used extensively in that country's automobile manufacturing industry. Similar examples can be found in other countries. There are often legitimate reasons for these different work practices (the availability of labour, length of production cycles, etc.). Work practices within the same industry also provide little commonality. Take hospitality work for instance. The requirements of food preparation and service vary across different kinds of hotels, motels, cafes and restaurants. Differences are found in the kind and degree of service, as well as in the processes and products of food preparation. The diverse cuisines provided in restaurants not only represent different culinary choices, they reflect distinct traditions of cooking techniques and principles.

Even vocational practice that might be considered more uniform—such as nursing or the work of motor mechanics—can differ widely according to where it is practised. Mechanics in major city dealerships engage in activities that are quite different from those in garages in small rural towns. Those working in dealerships probably learn to specialise in one or two makes of automobiles and much of their work might comprise servicing of vehicles that are just a few years old. Conversely, a mechanic in a small-town garage is more likely to have to service, maintain and repair different kinds, brands and ages of vehicles, and vehicles that serve a variety of functions (e.g. cars, trucks, buses, tractors). Whereas their city counterparts will be able to order replacement parts, the country mechanics may have to fabricate components and keep aging vehicles going long after the dealership warranty would have expired. However, the dealership mechanics may possess more specialised knowledge and be more conversant with current technology than their small-town counterparts. In a similar way, nurses in small regional hospitals are required to perform different tasks and roles from those in major teaching hospitals in capital cities. Again, breadth of activities may characterise nursing in smaller communities and the need to compensate for a shortage of doctors, whereas specialisation may be a key requirement for employment in a city teaching hospital. So the requirements for performance at work, and what constitutes everyday and new problems in these workplaces, are likely to be quite different, although bounded by common vocational practices.

Differences in the requirements for work extend beyond the purely technical nature of the activities. The scope for working autonomously, and the management of that work—its discretion—can vary widely. Also, whether work requires specialisation within a set of particular tasks or has more multi-functional roles will differ across and within workplaces. Nevertheless, the technical components of vocational practice determine part of the requirements for work performance. Therefore, although conceptions of occupations and industry are commonly used for categorising work skills, they alone are inadequate for providing a comprehensive account of the requirements for work performance. This is because the requirements of practice in particular workplaces are probably unique, given the range of factors that determine that practice (Billett 1998).

The changing nature of work practice

The nature of work and work practice is also constantly changing, thereby demanding fresh appraisals of what constitutes performance at work (Casey 1999). For instance, the use of technology has become so widespread that it is now accepted as a normal part of most people's work (Barley & Orr 1997). Technology both changes work and makes new demands on workers. 'The need to cope with operating systems, servers, networks and applications has clearly wrought a fundamental change in daily tasks' (Barley & Orr 1997: 8). For instance, operating computer numerically controlled (CNC) lathes requires different understandings and procedures than working with manually controlled lathes (Martin & Scribner 1991)—CNC lathe operators require high levels of conceptual and symbolic knowledge. This work now involves taking information from the 'blueprint' through to digitally programming the lathe to shape metal components. Similarly, Zuboff (1988) notes how the use of technology has separated workers from the actual workplace tasks. Hence their understanding of their work has become more abstract and has been displaced by a narrower range of perceptual tools. Procedures that are hidden, or unable to be observed and handled, are far more difficult to learn about. Changes in technology have also transformed the work of nurses (Cook-Gumperez & Hanna 1997) and bank workers (Hughes & Bernhardt 1999), providing enhanced discretion in some ways, while changing other components of work practice. Within the banking industry, technology has been used to organise jobs in different ways, up-skilling some tasks while automating, routinising or eliminating others (Hughes & Bernhardt 1999). Changes in work practice have also seen the centralisation or concentration of the management and organisation of work through electronic means. Production cycles are becoming shorter and more transformational (Wall & Jackson 1995), as are the means by which production occurs (Ellestrom 1998). Strategies of work rationalisation also bring changes to work (Ellestrom 1998). These changes require workers to respond to new tasks, to understand new concepts and develop new procedures—all of which make the work more demanding.

In his review of the changing nature of work, Bailey (1993) refers to accelerated production cycles, a proliferation of products, heightened levels of uncertainty and changing work practices. The consequences of such changes include the need to adapt to new situations, to manage the increased intensity of work as a result of greater competition, and to develop the capacity of workers to simultaneously engage in a number of demanding activities (Noon & Blyton 1997). Workers are also asked to embrace 'new' kinds of work organisation, such as teamwork, and to work with greater autonomy. However, such innovations are not uniformly adopted. Their implementation depends upon management perceptions of their utility (Darrah 1996). If, for instance, 'new' work practices are perceived as enhancing workers' control over work practice, then these 'new' practices may be avoided, modified or even dismantled by management, who may fear loss of control of production (Danford 1998). Consequently, identifying changes in work requirements cannot be undertaken at the industry or occupational level. How technology is applied, how the demands of changing work practice are manifested and identifying the changing organisation of work can best be understood at the workplace level, where these changes manifest themselves in particular work practice.

Overcoming assumptions about the requirements for work

The requirements for many kinds of work are probably underestimated. Understanding the demands of vocational practice, and how these are perceived, has a significant impact on the standing of the work and how expertise is valued. One legacy of Taylorism is the lowly standing of many vocations (Hull 1997). Taylorism involved ⊭ the breaking down of work tasks into small, routinised and de-skilled components—to separate the mental requirements from the manual performance of the task—in order to enhance management control over work tasks. Few would dispute the demands and complexity of work classified as 'professional' or 'technical'. However, although often unrecognised, similar demands are often a part of work labelled 'semi-skilled', 'unskilled' and 'operative'. Such work has been shown to require the ability to respond to new workplace tasks as often as professional occupations (Billett 1994a). The status of work influences how those undertaking work activities are permitted to engage in them, how their contributions are valued and the support and recognition their work attracts within the workplace (Darrah 1996, 1997; Hull 1997). Dewey (1916) has argued for the centrality of vocations to individuals' identity and well-being. He also concludes that when an occupation is viewed with contempt, it may have a detrimental effect on individuals. For example, historically determined distinctions between management and labour, professions and craft have resulted in assumptions about the roles, focus and discretion to be afforded to these kinds of work. Therefore, it is necessary to put to one side assumptions about categories of work and to attempt to understand the requirements of work on its own terms, not on the basis of untested assumptions.

Changes to participation in work

Changes to the ways in which individuals participate in work may make the task of learning about work more difficult. Changes such as those brought about by technology, or by work practices requiring greater discretion in decision-making, are making learning more difficult as well as making work more complex to perform. A study of bankers' work (Bertrand & Noyelle 1988) demonstrates how efforts to make operatives' work more routine had quite the opposite effect. Learning becomes more difficult when the worker is isolated from expertise likely to assist that learning. The absence of the support and guidance that was once accessible in the bank branch (e.g. managers, accountants) may make the task of learning banking procedures by tellers more difficult. They have to learn about bank telling through a narrower range of perceptual tools (Zuboff 1988) or via indirect means. This task is probably made even more demanding by the increasingly part-time nature of this workforce.

Part-time and home-based workers may face problems learning about work because their physical remoteness from the hub of current knowledge makes learning the requirements for work more difficult. They are often excluded from important information required for work performance. Significantly, the percentage of workers who are contractual and/or part-time—known as contingent workers—is growing in Europe (Forrester et al. 1995; Noon & Blyton 1997), the United States (Grubb 1996), Canada (Lipsig-Mumme 1996) and Australia. Being contingent may also make it difficult to access the knowledge required for performance in another way. Contemporary workplaces are often highly contested terrain (Billett 1999a). Access to participation in new workplace tasks, as well as opportunities to learn and be supported and guided, are not evenly distributed. Not all workers are welcomed or assisted to learn the requirements for work. Affiliations, gender, race, language, workplace cliques or the basis of employment (e.g. whether part-time or full-time) can marginalise workers. These workers may have to struggle to gain access to the activities and support required to develop expertise in such contested workplaces (Butler 1999; Probert 1999).

In sum, the requirements for expertise in the workplace cannot be reduced to understanding the bundle of technical skills required for performance (Berryman 1993). How vocational practice is conducted, the changes in that practice and the difficulties of learning the attributes required for responding to new tasks all have to be considered. At one level, vocations and the need for particular sets of skills are determined in the broader community (i.e. the need for particular goods and services) and will change as these needs evolve. However, these needs give rise to sets of understandings and procedures that characterise particular vocations. It is these vocations that provide a consistent line of work and development. However, some jobs require more than one set of vocational knowledge (e.g. fitters and turners, clerical workers in hospitals, vocational teachers). This again suggests that, as well as knowledge of the vocation, how that vocation is manifested in a particular workplace needs to be accounted for in understanding vocational expertise.

Consequently, to describe more fully the requirements for expertise at work, two sets of understandings need to be drawn upon and integrated. The first set comprises understandings about the knowledge required for performance. These are provided by the cognitive literature. Second, other literature describes the contributions of situations and the cultural practices of work. The next section describes and illustrates the forms of knowledge identified in the cognitive literature and the significance of their role in underpinning expertise.

THE COGNITIVE VIEW OF THE KNOWLEDGE UNDERPINNING PERFORMANCE

Over the past 30 years, cognitive psychology has attempted to identify the source of high levels of performance or expertise in individuals. Experts' ability to think and act is quite different from those who lack this capacity (i.e. novices). Therefore, much effort has been directed towards understanding how experts think and act by examining novice–expert differences. The breadth and organisation of individuals' knowledge is held to be a key determinant for expert performance. Rather than just being effective at processing information, the breadth and organisation of individuals' knowledge is held to be central to experts' successful performance. Cognitive theory proposes that individuals' knowledge resides in their memories and in different forms described as *cognitive structures*. This knowledge is what we use in our everyday activities. It is also deployed consciously in demanding activities such as dealing with new tasks and problem-solving, including transfer of knowledge to new applications (Anderson 1993; Stevenson et al. 1994). In turn, through its use, this knowledge is developed further. Therefore, cognitive activities such as learning, transfer and problem-solving are commonly associated with the use, testing and modification or development of these cognitive structures (Glaser 1990).

The usual distinctions are those between conceptual (propositional) and procedural forms of knowledge (Anderson 1982; Glaser 1984). However, cognitive structures and their deployment are inherently dispositional (Perkins et al. 1993). Therefore, to augment these categories of procedures and concepts, dispositions—such as interest, values and attitudes—need to be included (Prawat 1989; Perkins et al. 1993; Tobias 1994). Consequently, the term 'knowledge', as used here, encompasses conceptual and procedural forms of knowledge and the dispositions (values, attitudes) that underpin them. These different forms of knowledge are now described in more detail.

Propositional or conceptual knowledge

Propositional knowledge, or 'knowledge that' (Ryle 1949), is also known as *declarative knowledge* (Anderson 1982). It comprises facts, information, propositions, assertions and concepts. Levels of conceptual knowledge of increasing complexity differentiate propositional knowledge. These levels range from simple factual knowledge (e.g. names of pieces of equipment, tools or workplace procedures) through to deeper levels of conceptual knowledge, such as understanding about workings of a process at work, sets of procedures or pieces of equipment, or rich knowledge about the vocation.

The complexity of propositional knowledge is characterised in terms of its depth (Greeno 1989b). However, depth of understanding is premised on links and associations among concepts (Prawat 1989). Understanding how changes to one part of a production or information processing system will impact on other areas is an example of *depth of understanding*. This level of understanding can assist the completion of a new work task, its monitoring and judgments about the effectiveness of what has been done. For instance, hairdressers' understanding of hair structures informs them of the dangers of repeated use of chemicals in treating clients' hair. Also, their knowledge of chemical and heat treatments, supplemented by local knowledge about the client's likely care of hair from past treatments, will influence recommendations to clients. When undertaking a new task (non-routine activity), the problem-solver is often required to go beyond the surface features of the task to access its deep features (Gott 1989). The photocopier technician may use an understanding of the components of the machine to problem-solve by examining the components most likely to fail. So, within a particular vocational practice, deep conceptual knowledge enables complex problem-solving tasks through an understanding of the likely nature of the problem and its associations with other, related considerations. Depth of understanding within a vocation is probably limitless. This is because the factors that influence performance are interrelated in such complex ways as to ultimately be beyond human comprehension. Also, given the changing nature of vocational practice, what constitutes depth is constantly evolving.

Procedural knowledge, or 'knowledge how'

The knowledge that we use to act is referred to as *procedural knowledge* (Anderson 1982) or 'knowledge how' (Ryle 1949). Procedural knowledge comprises techniques, skills and the ability to secure goals (Stevenson 1994b). It is also classifiable into levels or orders (Evans 1991a; Stevenson 1991). Stevenson (1991) proposes three levels of orders. First-order or specific procedures are employed to achieve particular goals or tasks. Specific procedures are those we use without recourse to conscious thought. Examples might include an experienced electrician wiring a power point, clothing machinists threading their sewing machines, the use of save and filing functions in word processing, the changing of gears in a car or the placement of curling rods in clients' hair by an experienced hairdresser. However, being specific to particular tasks, these procedures cannot address new workplace tasks as they arise. Being able to hammer a nail does not permit you to consider what kind of nail would best be used for fastening a particular kind of new material (e.g. fibreboard). In these situations, second-order procedures—those that monitor and evaluate strategy selection—are invoked. These procedures can break work activity down into a series of sub-tasks (Greeno & Simon 1988) or engage in 'means–end' analysis—'in order to achieve ... I need to consider ...' (Newell & Simon 1972) to decide which approach to take to the job. Such a process means working out ahead of time what is required and what steps have to be taken to achieve the task. Hence the aircraft technician may work out the most efficient means to access a particular component in order to avoid stripping down a section of the plane to access it (Gott 1995). These first- and second-order procedures are postulated as being managed by a third or higher order of procedural knowledge (Evans 1991a; Stevenson 1991) which monitors and organises activities, and is strategic in its applications.

Higher order procedures are particularly important when we are faced with novel activities, such as complicated problem-solving or the transfer of knowledge to new situations. The illustrative examples at the beginning of this chapter required the experts to employ conscious and higher order procedures to organise, plan the work task, monitor its progress and predict likely outcomes. In doing so, action was being guided in a way different from the deployment of automated specific procedures (Simon & Simon 1978). This facility is necessary to respond to new requirements as they arise in workplaces. Being able to resolve these kinds of problems within an individual's vocational practice is a distinguishing quality of experts. '[T]he ability to perform successfully in novel situations is the hallmark of human cognition' (Anderson 1982: 391). It is these kinds of performances that establish particular individuals in the workplace as experts.

Dispositions

Concepts and procedures associated with a vocational practice are useful in the ways described above. However, some parts of behaviour cannot be explained fully by procedural and conceptual categories of knowledge. For instance, how can being pleasant to customers in a retail or restaurant setting, or the appropriateness of the level of checking and self-monitoring required of a motor mechanic, be categorised? These behaviours, probably best conceptualised as *dispositions*, comprise attitudes, values, affect, interests and identity (Prawat 1989) associated with work. Perkins et al. (1993) regard dispositions as individuals' tendencies to put their capabilities into action. Dispositions determine whether individuals value a work task enough to engage in the effortful process required to learn that knowledge. This consideration extends to their goals for participating in learning. For instance, students or workers may determine whether participation in an activity will result in them 'looking smart'. This is a quite different tendency from those who seek to determine what they will learn from a work activity before participating (Dweck & Elliot 1983). Dispositions determine more than the effort to be expended; they also impact on the organisation of what was learnt.

Workers will have preferences for particular work procedures based on what they have previously experienced from using different kinds of procedures. The significance of dispositions lies in the differences between what individuals are capable of doing and what tasks they actually undertake. Implicit beliefs about intelligence are held, with some individuals viewing intelligence as being predetermined and fixed, while others believe it can be developed further (Dweck & Leggett 1988). Similarly, workers' beliefs will likely influence how they approach effortful work activities. Some will see workplace learning arrangements only as occasions that will expose further their inherent weaknesses. Hence they may be reluctant to participate. Given the active role learners play in learning new knowledge, how they engage in particular tasks will influence what they learn from that task. Put simply, individuals are unlikely to engage enthusiastically in acquiring knowledge that they do not value.

Cultural values are also significant. Each vocation has particular values that are essential to its conduct. We expect our doctors to be discreet, our airline pilots to be cautious, our hospitality workers to be polite but not deferential, our teachers to be punctual. Again, these values will have different constructions in different workplaces. Hospitality workers in trendy cafes may be cool, while their counterparts in prestigious restaurants may be highly attentive. The learning of new vocational knowledge is unlikely to be supported by a workplace environment that does not value the particular knowledge (Lave 1990). Equally, cultural values may determine whether an effortful or superficial response to a task is likely to be warranted (Goodnow 1990). For instance, workers who are constantly asked to change their practice—apparently with no good reason—begin to treat such requests superficially. Consequently, dispositions have dimensions pertaining to individuals (their values, beliefs and attitudes), those of the vocation (the confidentiality of medical staff, the caution of pilots) and those pertaining to the particular values of the work practice. Together, these social, cultural and personal dispositional attributes contribute to the requirements for and learning of the vocational knowledge needed for performance.

Although they have been referred to separately above, it is important to emphasise the interdependence of these three forms of knowledge. Together, conceptual, procedural and dispositional representations offer a basis for understanding the kinds of knowledge required for performance from the cognitive view. The deployment and development of each cannot be understood fully without reference to the others (see Figure 2.1).

Figure 2.1   Interdependence of conceptual, procedural and dispositional knowledge

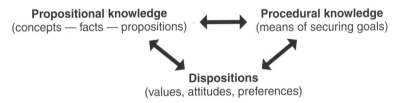

Propositional knowledge
(concepts — facts — propositions)

Procedural knowledge
(means of securing goals)

Dispositions
(values, attitudes, preferences)

For example, take the car journey referred to in the previous chapter. How the journey is conceptualised (propositional knowledge) by individuals is influenced by their attitude (dispositions) towards the tasks. Equally, concepts are evaluated through the applications of procedures (procedural knowledge)—the journey itself, which is underpinned by judgments about the worth of expending effort (dispositions) on this particular task of driving. These categorisations could be applied to any workplace task. The degree to which a computer technician believes that the owner should replace the computer with a new one will determine the advice they offer and the effort they engage in to repair the problem. Therefore, everyday thinking, acting and learning will interdependently engage and develop further all three of these forms of knowledge. Moreover, these forms of knowledge together help identify what constitutes vocational expertise.

THE COGNITIVE VIEW OF EXPERTISE

Research within cognitive psychology has focused on providing an account of complex human performance or expertise and how it is developed. Consequently, it provides a useful basis for understanding vocational expertise and the ways in which it can be developed at work. The research mainly comprises investigations of expert and novice differences within specific domains of activities. Importantly, this focus on specific domains assists in aligning the outcomes of this research directly to vocations (e.g. plumbing, electrical work, hairdressing, nursing). Through a synthesis of the literature on expert–novice differences, key attributes of experts' performance have been identified. These are: (a) effective categorisation of problems; (b) monitoring of problem resolutions; (c) instantaneous application of cognitive processes; (d) correct diagnosis of problems using principles; and (e) effective use of solution strategies. Descriptions of these attributes are useful in describing and prescribing the gap that needs to be closed between novices' or newcomers' abilities and those of experts. This is the task for learning in workplaces.

Effective categorisation of problems

Experts have the capacity to categorise tasks by the means of their solution. The doctor, upon diagnosing a patient, will quickly begin to form conclusions about what therapy is the most appropriate (Groen & Patel 1988). The hairdresser, on seeing the client walk into the salon, begins to consider the range of likely options they will suggest to the client, based on their appearance and existing hairstyle (Billett 1995a). Later, through negotiation, they may extend the options or be guided to discuss just one option. As a result of a rich repertoire of experiences in their vocation, the breadth and organisation of experts' knowledge permits this categorisation of problems by their means of resolution (Chi et al. 1981; Gott 1989; Sweller 1989). These experiences assist the practitioner to select the most viable or appropriate course of action for the workplace task. This facility is not always available to novices, particularly with problems that are new to them, as they have not developed the ability to categorise in this way. Depth of conceptual knowledge within a vocational domain also provides a basis for determining what is important or trivial in problem situations, thus aiding its resolution. For instance, an experienced motor mechanic may quickly identify whether the liquid dripping from a car exhaust is condensation or indicates something far more serious. Essentially, experts see different problems from those seen by novices and, because of their rich repertoire of experiences, are able to categorise problems by means of their solution (Gott 1988). Often novices are only able to respond to the problem's surface features (Sweller 1989) because they lack the expert's depth of understanding. When diagnosing a vehicle breakdown, the expert mechanic may quickly identify the cause and respond on the basis of hearing the engine, or identify its cause by a selective examination of some key components. In both cases, novices are less likely to be effective, as they lack the understanding and procedures to discern the nature of the problem and consider the most appropriate solution. So a key attribute of experts, in their domain of expertise, is to respond to a workplace problem by effectively categorising it in terms of its solution.

Monitoring of problem resolutions

Experts can also effectively monitor the task as it is being performed, and use that monitoring to assist in the task's successful completion. This monitoring comprises the expert testing and refining of their selected responses to a problem (Alexander & Judy 1988; Eylon & Linn 1988; Owen & Sweller 1989). Expert mechanics engaged in stripping down an engine actively monitor their progress in order to confirm their original diagnosis of the problem. If they discover something unanticipated (e.g. traces of water where it should not be), through that monitoring they are able to reappraise their original diagnosis and take action appropriate to what their monitoring has revealed. Guided by experts' rich base of domain-specific vocational knowledge, this monitoring permits a progressive evaluation of selected courses of action, and promotes the evaluation of alternative strategies for securing solutions (Glaser 1990). Monitoring also enables accurate judgments of the problem's complexity, the apportioning of time, assessments of progress and predictions of outcomes (Larkin et al. 1980; Chi et al. 1982). Underpinning this monitoring is the efficacy of the organisation of the individual's vocational knowledge. The breadth of experts' domain-specific knowledge, and its organisation, are products of participation in the vocation over a period of time. Again, this is a facility that is simply unavailable to novices, because they have not had the repertoire of experiences required to organise their knowledge around salient principles associated with their vocational practice.

Efficient and quick responses

Experts are also efficient and expeditious with their activities and energies. They are able to apply their cognitive processes instantaneously, because of their compiled procedural knowledge and chunked conceptual knowledge, in ways that allow routine activities to be accomplished 'automatically' (Ericsson & Simon 1984; Sweller 1989). As discussed in the previous chapter, compilation and chunking reduce cognitive load, thereby freeing the conscious memory to concentrate on unfamiliar components of the task. Therefore, through an extensive repertoire of experiences, the development of procedures and conceptual understanding permits the completion of familiar parts of the activity without recourse to conscious processing. Computer technicians will work quickly through various diagnostic processes in trying to resolve a problem in your computer's operating system. You have difficulty following their actions as they quickly scan the diagnostic information before moving on to the next screen. They know what they are looking for and will quickly identify settings that are aberrant through highly active monitoring. Also, because they have undertaken these tasks many times, they quickly and effortlessly shift from screen to screen. As they know these tools and screens well, their working or conscious memory is left to concentrate on unfamiliar parts of the activity. However, for novices, all or many parts of the activity may be new because they do not have the advantage of the kinds of compiled and chunked knowledge that expert computer technicians possess.

Correct diagnosis of problems using principles

Experts are also more likely than novices to be correct when faced with a novel workplace task. The deep conceptual knowledge of experts enables them to propose consistently correct diagnoses and responses to new or ill-defined problems (Gott 1988; Lesgold et al. 1989). If the task is wholly novel, the means of accomplishing it— or even the goal and place to start—may not be known. When requested to cook a new meal, the chef may be uncertain not only about the best process for cooking the meal, but also what the finished product should taste or look like. Substantial differences between experts' and novices' performance are evident in such situations (Gott 1988; Lesgold et al. 1989). Experts can extend their knowledge to close gaps in their available information and consistently produce more useful solutions than novices. Also, experts are more efficient with their search for problem solutions (Anderson 1982). One reason for this is that their knowledge is likely to be organised around important principles of the vocation. The expert chef has understanding associated with different approaches to cooking. These can be used to consider the new meal, and even discern the techniques of cooking used in an unfamiliar cuisine. Without this body of understanding and its organisation, conscious utilisation of higher order procedures would be required for task completion, which would limit the expert's ability by imposing a demanding cognitive load.

Effective solution strategies

As a product of their extensive learning experiences, experts' cognitive processes are 'debugged' through practice (Ericsson & Simon 1984; Glaser 1989, 1990). This facility assists the vocational expert to utilise their knowledge purposefully in responding to both familiar and new workplace tasks. When faced with new tasks, novices usually perform less well than experts, who rely on systematic and conscious solution searches (Glaser 1990). Experts use a goal-directed and tightly focused search of their vocational knowledge, deploying specific reasoning strategies such as stating arguments, seeking qualifications, using analogies and problem-solving strategies and rebutting counter-arguments (Voss et al. 1983; Gott 1988). The autoelectrician, in seeking to identify and isolate a faulty connection buried beneath the dashboard, will use their accumulated knowledge of wiring systems, testing in a logical and directed way until discovering the source and pathway around the connection. Again, because of domain-specificity, this search option may simply be unavailable to novice autoelectricians. In sum, these attributes describe how experts' thinking is different from that of novices. The attributes identified above importantly become the goals for learning and their development needs to become a key focus for evaluating and organising workplace learning experiences. These expert attributes are based on the breadth and organisation of their vocational knowledge. Comprising conceptual knowledge (both factual and deeper kinds), procedures (both specific and higher order) and the values appropriate for the vocation, these forms of knowledge need to be extensive enough and organised in ways that affect vocational practice and its performance in particular workplaces. So, beyond the ability to perform familiar work activities, experts also need to: (a) generate and evaluate skilled performance as technical tasks become complex and as situations and processes change; (b) reason and solve technical problems; (c) be strategic; (d) innovate; and (e) adapt (Stevenson 1994b). Through the identification of expert attributes, cognitive psychology has gone some way towards providing the goals for learning in the workplace. However, the domains of knowledge it refers to also need to account for the circumstances in which vocations are practised.

Situational factors of workplaces play an important role in determining the activities to be undertaken and the goals that are desirable in those workplaces. It is against these activities and goals that performances are judged, rather than some abstract notion of vocational competence. For example, it was shown that the requirements for performance across four hairdressing salons were quite different (Billett 1995a). In one salon, expertise was primarily associated with giving stylish cuts and colours, yet it also required the hairdresser to understand and use language and concepts that could be described as 'new age'. In another salon, expertise was focused on working as part of a large team, knowing which part of the hairdressing task could best utilise the competence of each hairdresser. It also included managing clients' hairdressing needs while tempting them with additional treatments that would boost the salon's revenue. Yet continuity of the clientele was also important, so care was taken not to surprise or burden clients with additional and unacceptable costs. In a third salon, being able to manage 'awkward' customers, while maintaining their confidence, was an important attribute of managing the hairdressing tasks. In a fourth salon, the clientele comprised mainly elderly ladies. Here, expertise was associated as much with being knowledgeable about the clients' families and being a friend and confidant to these often lonely clients, as providing what would be seen in other salons as fairly routine hair treatments. So the vocational practice of hairdressing manifested itself quite differently in each of these salons. In doing so, it presented quite different goals and bases for performance. Also, in terms of dispositions, it is unclear whether some hairdressers would be able to work in some of the other salons or whether they would even be interested in doing so. Their vocational values (e.g. transforming clients' appearances) determine how they would participate in each of these salons.

The phenomenon identified here is not restricted to hairdressing. Consider the example of the differences between activities required to be undertaken by mechanics in the city dealership or garage in a small rural town mentioned earlier. Consider also the different requirements for chefs working in a banquet kitchen of a five-star hotel, its bistro, the cafe in the trendy suburb, the hospital kitchen, officers' mess, mining camp or kitchen manufacturing meals for airline passengers. Think also of the different roles undertaken by nurses in a major teaching hospital, a small-town hospital, workplaces, a remote Indigenous community, caring for the aged in nursing homes or providing care for patients in their own homes. So, in terms of examining the requirements for performance as goals for learning, it is necessary to consider how workplace factors shape requirements for vocational performance.

SITUATING EXPERTISE IN WORKPLACES

Following on from this, the requirements for work can only be fully understood in terms of actual work practice. It is not possible to ignore situational requirements, nor is it appropriate to deny the vocational concepts and procedures that are more widely applicable. Vocational practice, and hence expertise, need to be understood and judged in terms of the reality of everyday work practices because they are what furnish the problems, the goals and their solutions. Whereas somebody might be viewed as being an expert in one workplace, they might be judged as a novice or as indulgent in another because their responses to the particular workplace tasks are inappropriate. However, it is also important to consider the essential practices that characterise the vocation. It might be preferable for vocational practitioners to extend their skills into other workplaces that conduct the same vocational activities. However, as noted, there will be differences in the extent to which their knowledge can or should be transferred to situations or activities that are marked by difference. A workplace curriculum has to attempt to embed expertise in the dynamic and unique practice of the workplace and develop the capacities of workers to respond to new vocational tasks, including transfer to other tasks or workplace settings.

Cognitive theory suggests that the ability to transfer depends in part on the degree of congruence between the organisation of individuals' constructions of knowledge and the commonality of aspects of the situation to which it is being applied (Pea 1987). This is supported by Royer's (1979) concept of 'near' and 'far' transfer, discussed earlier (see Chapter 1). The target for transfer to another situation, whether 'far' or 'near', will be determined by similarities between the two circumstances as perceived by the individual. Elements of the vocational practice that are enduring (e.g. specific procedures, such as wiring power points, techniques for preparing and cutting food, using a keyboard) may make transfer 'near'. However, more specific requirements of the workplace (e.g. typing particular types of correspondence, preparing particular kinds of food) may make the transfer of what was learnt in one workplace 'far'. As workplaces are likely to be differentiated by factors that shape their practice, expertise will be conceptualised differently across workplaces, even when the same vocational practice is being undertaken. There will be common elements, yet how this work is conducted is likely to be situational to a greater or lesser degree.

Therefore the situational dimensions of expertise involve going beyond the insights provided by cognitive psychology to utilise those that account for social and cultural contributions to thinking, acting and performance. Propositions advocated by Lave and Wenger (1991) and Wenger (1998) provide useful starting points. What they define as a community of practice is analogous to work practice. They refer to full participation in a community of practice, rather than to expertise (Lave 1991). Their concept of full participation is shaped by a belief that all practitioners are peripheral because work practice is inevitably constantly evolving. Lave and Wenger (1991) maintain that learning in a community of practice (e.g. 'workplace) is shaped through the process of becoming a full participant in that practice (Lave & Wenger 1991). Consequently, engagement in the workplace, over time, is necessary for learning the knowledge required to become a full participant and embracing the identity of the vocation. This is consistent with what was proposed within the cognitive view of expertise about the need for access to extensive experience to compile debugged procedures and chunk concepts.

By referring to full participation, expertise is seen to relate to participation in particular workplaces. This view also emphasises the need to move from peripheral to full participation within that practice. However, it also proposes that work practice is constantly transforming. Full participation implies 'being capable with new activities, performing new tasks and comprehending new understanding' (Lave & Wenger 1991: 53) in the workplace. This requirement responds to the need for attributes of expertise to be adaptable and transferable. Individuals are defined by, and may also actively define, the relationship (Lave & Wenger 1991). This means that individual workers in some ways shape the requirements for work. The reciprocal nature of engagement in work practice and appropriation of knowledge is emphasised in this view. However, novices may contest or challenge existing assumptions and, through their participation, change the practice (Hodges 1998). So, rather than learning as participation in the social practice of work being socialisation or enculturation, those on the pathway to full participation engage in contest and challenge, and ultimately may change the work practice.

In short, the performance requirements for work activities (and problems) are locatable within each workplace or work practice. Some problems will be significant, whilst others are trivial. In the trendy salon, being a confidante to lonely elderly ladies is less significant than in the salon where these clients are the core of the business. Finally, some skills and some areas of knowledge are seen in some communities as belonging to certain people more than others. For instance, in Darrah's (1997) study of a computer manufacturing company, the design engineers were seen as having a creative and problem-solving role. However, the production staff had to be highly adaptive and flexible to maintain levels of production. This was largely ignored and certainly not recognised within the company. In these kinds of ways, the workplace community determines a hierarchy of tasks and the privileging of those tasks (Lave 1990); within that privileging, there may be knowledge reserved for particular groups. Accordingly, this may inhibit access for others who are not appropriately affiliated, who are outside particular cliques, or whose gender, race or ethnicity attracts hostility and/or diminished opportunities to participate (Hull 1997). There may be legitimate reasons for restricting access to knowledge. For example, in two of the four hairdressing salons referred to earlier (Billett 1995a), the manager-owners were the only persons permitted to distribute and order the stock. It was claimed that if other staff had access to stock, it would be squandered and the businesses would not survive. However, in another salon, where owner-managers were also present, it was the apprentice's job to manage and order the stock. So there is likely to be a particular privileging of knowledge in each workplace, depending on its norms and practices.

To synthesise these situational factors into a comprehensive account of expertise at work, the following list of characteristics has been identified (Billett 1998). Expertise as conceptualised in the cognitive literature, with its focus on the skilful use of knowledge by experts, is subsumed within this view of expertise. The key characteristics are its relational, embedded, competent, reciprocal and pertinent characteristics, as follows:

- Expertise is *relational* in terms of requirements of a particular workplace or work practice. The requirements for performance are best understood in terms of the conceptual, procedural and dispositional components of knowledge of how the occupational practice or practices are manifested in the particular workplace.

- Expertise is *embedded* (being the product of particular sets of needs) with meaning about practice derived from becoming a full participant, over time and with understanding shaped by participation in the activities and norms of that practice. Learning about and becoming an expert requires lengthy engagement with the practice.

- Expertise requires *competence* in the community's discourse, in the routine and non-routine activities of practice, mastery of new understanding and the ability to perform and adapt existing skills. So expertise at work is more than 'technical' skills; it is how those skills are manifested in the workplace's activities, norms and values.

- Expertise is *reciprocal*, shaping and being shaped by the community of practice and those who participate in it. Those who are experts (full participants) are able to transform the practice. Their response to novel problems determines the direction of the workplace and shapes its development.

- Expertise requires *pertinence* in the appropriateness of problem solutions, such as knowing what behaviours are acceptable, and in what circumstances, in problem-solving. This quality reflects the values a workplace assigns to problems, their solutions, the appropriateness of the effort required and understanding of what knowledge is privileged (Billett 1998).

These characteristics emphasise the situatedness of vocational expertise and the likely need to participate extensively in that work practice in order to develop expertise that will be recognised in the workplace.

SUMMARY

The effectiveness of workplaces as learning environments should be judged on the basis of their ability to develop vocational expertise as outlined above. These can be summarised as follows. There is a need for conceptual, procedural and dispositional attributes to be developed that will permit performance in everyday tasks in the particular workplace setting. However, workplace learning experiences need to go beyond developing the requirements for everyday or routine workplace activities. They also need to develop the attributes required to respond to the non-routine tasks likely to be encountered in the workplace. It is accepted that some tasks will be too novel to reasonably expect even an expert to respond immediately. However, more than being the hallmark of expertise from the cognitive perspective, this ability and the need to for it to be maintained by ongoing learning acknowledges the ever-changing requirements for performance at work, and hence expertise.

The development of expert attributes is in the interest of enterprises that employ vocational practitioners, as well as of the practitioners themselves. They provide a basis for developing a workforce that is likely to be adaptable to the changing demands of work practice. Changes in work practice are as certain as the need to be able to adapt to them in order to sustain currency in vocational practice. Expert attributes in its workforce provide the enterprise with a basis to be confident about its capacity to respond to change. These attributes also furnish workers with the capacity to maximise their potential in achieving important personal and vocational goals. So, more than being focused on just achieving enterprise goals—as with provisions from educational institutions—the workplace has the potential to secure for individuals the capacity to realise the goals for their vocational practice.

These attributes are required in the workplace for workers to advance toward expertise, and transfer their vocational knowledge to new situations and other work environments. These measures provide the most useful basis for the selection of strategies to develop that knowledge and may therefore be used to demonstrate the efficacy of workplaces as learning environments.

3

Learning vocational expertise at work

UNDERSTANDING WORKPLACE LEARNING

Understanding the way people learn through participation at work is important for deciding how to best structure workplace learning experiences. The more this learning process is understood, the more focused efforts to develop vocational expertise in the workplace can be. Drawing on studies of learning in workplaces, this chapter identifies and discusses those factors likely to promote the development of expert performance at work and also those likely to hinder its development. The strengths and weaknesses of learning at work are identified, using evidence drawn largely from a series of research projects that specifically aimed to understand learning in the workplace and how it might be improved. These investigations progressively developed and refined an understanding of how workers learn through their work activities and of the strategies that could be used to improve learning that occurs as part of everyday work activities. This provides the basis for a workplace curriculum.

The first research project examined how workers in six open

cut coal mines had learnt their knowledge of coal mining (Billett 1993a, 1994a). In the open cut coal mining industry, there are few formalised courses for production workers, such as apprenticeships or pre-vocational preparation through colleges. The research project attempted to understand how, in the absence of courses, these workers had learnt their work. It was concluded that the context of the workplace was important for determining what was worth learning and how these workers had learnt. In particular, the significance of 'just doing it' (everyday work activities) and the support and guidance that the workplace provided—particularly from other coal workers—were identified as being significant sources of learning for these coal miners, as were observing and listening to other workers. Interestingly, tradeworkers at the mine sites also supported these findings. This was surprising, because the apprenticeship preparation of tradeworkers, which includes college-based experience, sets them apart from production workers in the coal mines. However, they also claimed to have learnt at work in similar ways, despite such claims undermining some of the distinctiveness these workers enjoyed in the workplace.

The second research project sought to determine whether the findings from the coal mines were applicable to other industry sectors. Surveys and lengthy interviews of workers across a range of industries (e.g. hospitality, transport, retail, warehouse, clerical, secondary processing) were used to determine how workers in these industries had learnt their work and understood the qualities of their learning experiences at work (Billett 1993b, 1994a). The findings supported and advanced further the findings of the coal workers' study. There was wide agreement across these industries that engagement in workplace activities, the direct guidance of other workers, observing workplace practices and the kinds of work tasks that workers undertook were central to learning about work. However, workers in these industry sectors also identified a consistent set of concerns about learning in workplaces. These included gaining access to experts and activities and, particularly, the difficulties of learning conceptual knowledge through everyday work experiences. Indeed, developing understanding through workplace experiences emerged as a clear and consistent concern.

Taking these findings further, the next investigation comprised a more detailed analysis of learning in just one enterprise—a secondary processing plant and mine site—over a five-month period. This investigation compared the processes and outcomes of everyday learning in the workplace with those provided through an in-house training system (Billett 1994b). Using 'critical incident' techniques in interviews, this study aimed to understand what had contributed to particular learning episodes at work. The data yielded further and more detailed evidence of the workplace's contribution to learning. This was achieved through identification of the relative potency of the 'learning curriculum' (everyday learning) compared with the taught curriculum (the training system) in this workplace. The following investigation comprised a detailed inquiry of four workplaces (hairdressing salons) and how and what individuals (hairdressers and novice hairdressers) learnt in those workplaces (Billett 1995a, 1996a). The hairdressing study provided a finer analysis of how learning occurred and the relationship among the workplace activities, the workplace itself and what individuals learnt. Two further investigations were subsequently undertaken to evaluate the effectiveness of particular interventions that aimed at improving learning in the workplace. The first evaluated strategies aimed at developing conceptual knowledge in hospitality workplaces (Billett & Rose 1999). The second evaluated the use of guided learning strategies in five workplaces (Billett et al. 1998). The first four investigations are referred to extensively in this chapter.

WORKPLACE ACTIVITIES AND GUIDANCE: CONTRIBUTIONS TO DEVELOPING EXPERTISE

The contributions of workplaces to learning vocational practice can be classified broadly as those associated with the activities individuals engage in and those related to the support and guidance they receive while undertaking work activities. As previewed in Chapter 1, routine and non-routine workplace tasks, the guidance provided by other workers, the indirect contributions of other workers and the support provided by the workplace all contribute to learning at work, albeit in different ways. Other investigations of workplace learning (e.g. Owen 1995, 1999; Ballenden 1996; Harris et al. 1996a; Harris et al. 1996b; Harris & Volet 1996, 1997; Volkoff 1996; Harris & Simons 1999) largely uphold these propositions. In different ways, these investigations propose that the kinds of activities individuals engage in, and the support or access they receive, influence the development of their work-related knowledge. The direct guidance of others (experts and peers) provides models, mentors and clues about performance and also assists in developing understanding that workers would not learn alone. Indirect guidance provided by other workers (e.g. comparing, listening and observing) (Harris et al. 1996a; Harris & Simons 1999) and the physical environment (the workplace, its tools, etc.) (Billett 1994a; Billett et al. 1998) provide visual clues that aid our thinking and learning. This type of guidance is unlikely ever to be provided through textbooks or through engagement in non-authentic activities, such as simulated tasks and those disembedded from practice (e.g. those in classroom settings).

Evidence of the effectiveness of these contributions to learning is found in data from three of the investigations previewed above. In the coal mining study (Billett 1993a), workers at three mines responded to a survey based on an earlier round of interviews at three other mines about what contributions had been useful to their learning of coal mining in the workplace. When asked to rate these contributions, 98 per cent of these workers reported 'just doing it' and 86 per cent 'other workers' as being either 'quite effective' or 'very effective'. These responses were far higher than for 'external providers' of training, for instance. Taken from the third study, Table 3.1 presents a summary of the data of how secondary process workers learnt in their workplace (Billett 1994b). Data about the contributions to their learning were gathered over a five-month period using a 'critical incident' technique. Every four weeks, workers were asked to describe situations where they: (a) had been able to complete a new task; (b) had difficulty and required assistance for task completion; and (c) were unable to complete a task. Having recounted these incidents, they identified and rated the contributions to: (i) their learning to complete the tasks; (ii) the contributions that were required for them ultimately to be successful with those tasks

Table 3.1   Contributions to learning during critical incidents

Aid to learning	5[1]	4	3	2	1[1]
A Learning guides	6[3]	1	3	1	6[3]
B Computer-based learning		1		1	4[2]
C Video					2[2]
D Mentors	15[2]	7	8	1	2
E Direct instruction	17[2]	9	9	3	3
G Observing and listening	30[2]	10	3	5	2
H Other workers	22[2]	7	17	3	
F Everyday activities	21[2]	8	11	5	3
I Work environment	11[3]	11[3]	10	4	3

Notes:
1 Rating from 5 to 1 = very useful through to not useful
2 Mode
3 Bimodal

Source: Billett (1994b)

they required assistance with; and (iii) the contributions that were lacking in those situations where they were unsuccessful. Table 3.1 presents a summary of these findings and weightings of the contributions. The in-house training system (i.e. learning guides, computer-based learning, videos) was consistently reported as being less effective than the contributions provided through undertaking everyday work activities. 'Observing and listening', 'other workers', 'everyday activities' and 'direct instruction' were consistently supported as effective in developing work-related knowledge. Even the contributions of the 'work environment'—the workplace itself—were rated higher than most of the contributions of the in-house training system in this workplace.

Table 3.1 presents evidence of the contributions of the 'learning curriculum'—those components of learning that take place through everyday work activity. As shown, these were consistently reported as being of greater utility than the 'teaching curriculum' (the in-house training system) in this study. It was also concluded that higher order procedural knowledge, which is seen as being essential for expert performance, was developed through the contributions reported as being most effective in Table 3.1. These findings are consistent with those from the study of coal miners' learning. They are also

Table 3.2 Learners' responses to critical incidents

Subject	Utility of learning curriculum						Utility of strategy				
	Mentor support	Activities	Observing and listening (mentor)	Observing and listening (others)	Workplace	Other workers	Questioning	Coaching	Analogies	Diagrams	Modelling
A1	3	**8**	1	4	**7**	2	0	0	0	0	0
A2	7	**11**	**9**	**9**	6	7	7	6	3	1	3
A3	10	**12**	**11**	2	8	8	9	10	6	8	**11**
A4	**10**	**10**	7	5	**9**	7	**9**	**10**	7	1	**9**
A5	**11**	**12**	8	7	9	7	10	6	2	1	1
A6	9	**10**	6	**11**	**10**	8	7	9	2	2	7
B7	7	**11**	3	2	**8**	5	3	3	1	0	1
B8	7	**12**	6	**10**	8	**12**	7	4	6	0	5
B10*	5	4	3	**7**	4	5	**6**	2	3	1	5
C11	2	**8**	2	**8**	7	**9**	2	2	2	0	0
D16	**8**	**9**	**8**	5	6	4	5	6	1	2	8
E17	**5**	**6**	1	**6**	4	**6**	3	3	2	2	2
E18	**4**	**6**	3	**4**	1	3	0	2	0	1	1
E19	3	2	**4**	**6**	1	**4**	0	1	0	1	0
E20	5	**8**	4	**8**	**7**	**8**	4	4	3	4	4
E21	4	**10**	4	**8**	**8**	5	4	3	0		1
E22	2	**7**	1	4	**6**	**6**	1	1	0		0
E23	3	**5**	**5**	**4**	3	**4**	**4**	2	0		3
E24	**10**	**9**	**9**	**10**	4	8	7	8	5	0	5
E25	7	**10**	7	**11**	5	8	8	6	3	0	2
E26	3	**7**	3	**7**	4	**6**	1	2	0	0	3
E27	2	**5**	2	**5**	4	**6**	1	2	2	2	2
Total	127	**172**	107	**142**	129	138	98	92	48	26	70

Note: * Subject B10—only three interviews were conducted, no subject B9 existed, subjects C12, C13, C14, C15 were omitted as the data sets were incomplete
Source: Billett et al. (1998)

consistent with an investigation of guided learning in five enterprises (Billett et al. 1998), where strategies were trialled to assist workplace learning (modelling, coaching, questioning, diagrams and analogies). Data about the effectiveness of the different kinds of contributions to learning were gathered through 'critical incidents' over a six-month period in each of these workplaces. Again, the effectiveness of everyday work activities was clearly evident. In Table 3.2, the left-hand column indicates the subject, while the columns to the right are organised under two headings (utility of the 'learning curriculum' and utility of strategies). These headings are used to categorise responses into those referring to everyday participation in the workplace and those responses to the strategies being trialled. A summary is presented of each learner's responses to the contributions to learning in each row. In the column, the sum of the number of times learners rated a contribution to their resolution of a work problem as 3, 4 or 5 is recorded. For ease of analysis, the two highest scores for each subject are bolded (e.g. **10 9**) and the two lowest underlined (e.g. 0 1). As can be seen, over all subjects and sites, 'everyday work activities', 'observing and listening to others' and 'other workers' were reported most frequently as having the strongest utility. The three lowest frequencies were reported for 'diagrams' (lowest), 'analogies' and 'modelling'.

Significantly, none of the 'strategy' categories was reported as being more effective than the 'learning curriculum' categories. This finding again suggests that everyday activity in the workplace provided the contributions that the subjects required for their work. However, perhaps the comparative strengths of learning in the workplace are not so surprising given the nature of, and requirements for, participation in everyday work activities. This participation provides ongoing and persistent opportunities for individuals to learn the knowledge required for work through their engagement in goal-directed workplace activities. Learning through doing at work is almost inevitable. Further, embedding learning in authentic work activities enriches it (Harris & Simon 1999). It is also ongoing—ever-present in everyday activities. However, while learning through work is inevitable, the concern is whether this kind of learning will result in the development of vocational expertise. To address this concern, it is necessary to understand in some detail the workplace learning process. Accordingly, an elaboration of the contributions to learning presented in Table 3.1 and 3.2 is provided in the sections below, which examine (a) engagement in work tasks; (b) the close guidance of other workers and experts; and (c) indirect guidance provided by the setting and the practice within that setting. Together, these contributions provide a basis for understanding learning in the workplace and the likely development of knowledge required for work through everyday activities.

Engagement in work activities: 'Just doing it'

> Because you are there in the actual store, when you are faced with day-to-day problems you learn because it is on-the-spot training.

> You learn to work on a client from day one. If you make a mistake, well it can all come down on you . . . because it was a client you were working on.

> The Station Mistress would let you do it yourself. I think I learnt a lot more doing that than at gate school.

> Trial and error has a lot to do with it. If you make a mistake you always remember how what you did was wrong. (All quotes from Billett 1994b.)

The coal miners in the first study (Billett 1993a) frequently stated that 'just doing it' was how they had acquired their vocational knowledge in the workplace. This apparently simple response captures a number of contributions to learning. When pressed further, some of these workers reported that their participation in work tasks had required them to engage in the kinds of thinking and acting from which they had learnt their work skills. That is, they had learnt through engagement in goal-directed work activities. These tasks had permitted them to learn new knowledge and reinforce further what they already knew. Through their engagement in workplace tasks, workers have to consider these tasks and determine how they will proceed with them. Hence they have embraced goal-directed activities that require problem-solving. These learning processes are authentic—they are set in the particular work practice where the tasks are undertaken, thereby making the learning applicable to that situation. When encountering a new task, workers have to consider and generate possible ways of approaching that task. Then they proceed with the approach they believe will produce the desired outcome. As they do this, they test, appraise the effectiveness of what they have proposed and modify their approach. Through practice, they can improve the effectiveness of their procedures. Over time, and with repeated practice, these tasks come to be completed with less effort through compilation. Similarly, through practice, the facts and concepts associated with goals and sub-goals of the task become richly associated, thereby assisting the purposeful organisation of their knowledge.

For example, in the furnace room at the secondary processing plant, the replacement of a carbon electrode required careful positioning and linking to the existing electrode. There was an optimum position for and length of the existing electrode that made the attachment of the new electrode easier. Also, two types of electrodes were being used, one of which was reputed to be more difficult to attach. The electrodes were quite brittle. Through practice, the workers learnt the timing and positioning for an optimum changeover, the care required in the attachment process, differences in handling the kinds of electrodes used and how the crane had to be deployed to gently position the replacement electrode. Through practice in workplace activities such as this, a worker's repertoire of concepts and the procedures required for work can gradually be developed. This learning activity is purposeful, as it leads to knowledge being constructed, reinforced, integrated and organised in ways likely to be effective for workplace tasks. Individuals also experience satisfaction when they adapt their existing knowledge structures through competent performance—or put more simply, when they are able to make sense of what they experience and demonstrably achieve success (von Glasersfeld 1987). Also, engagement in everyday work tasks helps reinforce the procedures used and the goals required for their performance.

The evidence suggests that everyday work—'just doing it'—
engages workers in an active and constructive process of learning
through their participation in goal-directed activities. As well as
developing specific forms of knowledge (e.g. specific procedures,
factual knowledge), this process is also conducive to developing the
kinds of higher orders of procedural knowledge and deeper conceptual knowledge that are required for expert performance (Billett
1994b, 1995b; Stevenson & McKavanagh 1994). This is because the
individual has had to identify and select ways of performing the task
and then monitor and test those means. The kinds of understandings
and procedures generated through such activities are the basis for
the transfer of vocational knowledge to other and new work tasks.
However, despite this, there are legitimate concerns that knowledge
learnt in workplaces might not be transferable elsewhere. The
process of transfer is not just about redeploying skills regardless of
context—across so many unconnected 'lily pads', to use Lave's
(1991) term. The kinds of activities through which learning occurs
and their similarity to other activities are also likely determinants of
the prospect of transfer.

Work that is more commonly practised, such as trade work (e.g.
fitters, hairdressers, plumbers) may provide a greater range of opportunities for application and transfer. However, for the production
worker in a specialised practice such as a copper refinery, a sugar
mill, an aluminium refinery or a workplace where patent equipment
is used, there may simply be fewer opportunities for transferring
knowledge to another workplace. Indeed, with such workplace tasks
and uniquely applicable procedures, the workplace may be the best
(perhaps the only) site to develop vocational knowledge that will
be more or less transferable (Harris & Volet 1996, 1997). Moreover,
shared learning arrangements across workplaces and educational institutions can have a positive impact on the learning outcomes (Harris
et al. 1996a, 1996b). Harris and his colleagues found that workplace
experiences assisted understanding of the value of the knowledge
being learnt in college environments. Students with prior workplace
experiences also had a 'head start' on other students. In these
ways, everyday activities in the workplace—'just doing it'—provide
a basis to develop the robust knowledge required for workplace

performance. However, more than mere engagement in work activities, direct and indirect forms of guidance in the workplace are required to develop the kinds of knowledge required for performance at work.

Guidance by other workers and experts

Problems are always discussed by the workers and it seems the best way to share experiences and solve problems.

You are able to learn from others ... these people are the source of experience and practical knowledge

In the control room. There's lots of talk going on. About different things that are happening. Is that useful? Yeah. If you know what they're talking about. If you don't know ... I just wait till they finish talking and then ask them what was this and what was that. (All quotes from Billett 1994b.)

The contribution of direct assistance and support (guidance) by more experienced coworkers provides a significant basis for learning. This assistance manifests itself in a number of different forms. More experienced coworkers can identify and select work tasks appropriate to learners' level of workplace competence or *readiness*. They can provide explanations where appropriate, and guide and monitor workers as they undertake new workplace tasks. The evidence suggests that this support and guidance is more or less accessible in most workplaces.

In workplaces where guidance is readily accessible, more experienced coworkers are able to guide the selection of those work tasks that are appropriate to the learners' level of development. The management of learners' access to increasingly more accountable tasks and assistance with their completion has been identified as making significant contributions to learning in the workplace (Billett 1994a; Ballenden 1996; Darrah 1997; Billett et al. 1998). The organisation of these experiences provides an important basis for structuring learning through work. Workplace learners report that, when more experienced coworkers understand and meet their needs, significant support for their learning is provided (Billett 1993b; Billett et al. 1998). Direct interactions with more experienced coworkers are reported as guiding learners' selection of approaches to workplace tasks and the monitoring of being successful with these tasks (Billett 1994b; Harris et al. 1996a). These interactions include telling, explaining and making explicit what would otherwise remain unknown by learners. Experts can provide assist by providing 'tricks of the trade' and heuristics (problem-solving strategies) that learners are unlikely to discover independently (Billett 1993b, 1994b). In these ways, guidance by more experienced workers provides models, clues and explanations for how to succeed with and refine performance with workplace tasks (e.g. how a task is completed, to what degree and to how high a standard).

During the commissioning phase of the secondary processing plant, production staff reported working with the overseas engineers from the company that had designed and manufactured the plant (Billett 1994b). The production workers engaged in joint activities with these experts in the construction and commissioning of the plant. Through these activities, the production workers learnt about the plant and how it best operated. This learning included the capacity to understand and respond to production problems. Later, through experience, it extended to refinements to the plant's operation required by changes in the kinds of ore being processed and its characteristics. Beyond modelling how the tasks should be undertaken, there were other important contributions. In particular, the process of engaging in shared workplace tasks with the engineers resulted in the production workers understanding how to operate the plant.

Significantly, in work situations where more experienced workers are unavailable—such as with workers who are physically isolated or who work alone—some workers actively seek out expert support. The investigation of learning across a range of industry sectors (Billett 1993b, 1994a) provided some examples. Working in a remote community, a national parks officer used telecommunications to contact an experienced colleague in another state to gain advice on how to proceed with workplace tasks. Although other people were more easily accessible, this worker valued the contributions of this expert colleague. In the same investigation, a beautician who worked alone attended cosmetic companies' product nights to meet with other beauticians to exchange ideas. Again, this was more than just contact with others—it was about accessing other knowledgeable workers.

Experts and other workers assist the learning of vocational knowledge through shared workplace activity. Some of this learning is of the kind that learners would not discover alone. The contribution of this shared or collaborative learning is found in the Vygotskian concept of interactions between individuals (inter-psychological processes) that are the basis of individuals' learning (intra-psychological outcomes), as discussed in Chapter 1. It is proposed that the scope of individuals' learning is likely to be greater when assisted by more experienced workers. Guiding a novice in achieving improved performance with a work task is a specific contribution that close guidance can provide in the workplace.

In summary, some of the contributions of direct guidance are similar to what is expected of teachers (e.g. telling, direct instruction). However, it is the expert coworker's ability to guide, organise and support the learning of the less experienced worker when engaged in work activities that is more important. This contribution comes through the shared problem-solving which extends to monitoring tasks, understanding needs and responding to those needs in ways that engage workplace learners in learning for themselves. The particular outcomes provided by close guidance are associated with the development of procedures required for successfully completing workplace tasks and assisting the learning of concepts and the development of understanding that individuals would not be able to achieve alone. The kinds of guidance provided by experts are analogous to the modelling, coaching and scaffolding referred to as cognitive apprenticeships (Collins et al. 1989). This approach to workplace learning, and strategies that specifically aim to develop conceptual knowledge in the workplace, are referred to in more detail in Chapter 5. However, beyond the contributions of direct guidance by experts, the workplace also provides other and less direct forms of assistance to learning.

Indirect guidance in the workplace

We could actually see the job that was being done . . . and we used the skills each and every day of our working lives, which is much easier than being taught. (Quoted in Billett 1994b.)

A barmaid reported that seeing customers in the context of the bar in which they drank and where she worked helped her remember which drinks they and their friends preferred (Billett 1994c). This was important to her, as good service prompted tips that augmented her low hourly rate of pay. However, away from the bar, she would be unable to recall the customers' preferred drinks. The workplace environment provides forms of guidance for learning that make a rich contribution to learning. These contributions come from observing and listening to other workers and the physical environment. Scribner (1997/1984) claims that the work environment is more than an external context: it is an integral component of the thinking and acting processes required for work. The term 'indirect' is used here to distinguish between the close guidance of the learner by a more expert other, as outlined in the previous section, and assistance to learning provided indirectly in the workplace. Two forms of indirect guidance were reported frequently in the studies into workplace learning. The first comprised the contributions provided indirectly by other workers. These included an expert coworker, peer or other worker being observed or listened to while conducting work tasks, or discussing these tasks with other workers. The second consisted of the contributions of the physical work environment. Along with Lave's (1990) study of tailors' apprentices and Bransford et al.'s (1985 cited in Pea 1987) description of spectacular learning in children, workers in the workplace learning studies also referred to learning through assistance from other workers and the physical workplace environment.

Listening to and observing other workers was consistently reported as helping learners to understand the goals for and processes of workplace tasks (Billett 1993b, 1994b; Billett et al. 1998). Much of this contribution is through the provision of models of how best to proceed. Clerical workers commented on observing colleagues' ways of dealing with customers as a basis for how they should proceed with the task (Billett 1993b). The valuing of this kind of assistance was not restricted to novices. Experienced workers also referred to observing and listening to other workers as a means of keeping up with the changing requirements of the workplace (Billett 1993a, 1994b). These contributions are available through everyday interactions. For instance, meal breaks were often mentioned as opportunities to learn in this way. This kind of interaction was identified particularly among members of the self-managed teams at the secondary processing plant. Workers there were able to detail situations in which they learnt in this way:

> Well, we've got some tradesmen that've been around for a long time. They are a very skilled group of people. Watching and learning from them is good.

> When Steve's talking to any of the other guys, I sort of listen in. I normally draw something on the board—that's got to do with the multi hearth. I just look and listen to whatever is going around. You know, just look and listen.

> I'm always listening to the two-way [radio]. And I'm always listening to what's going on. And what they're doing to solve the problem. [I] have a listen and then I go over and ask the bloke what was going on. You know, I say what were you doing over there? Were you having trouble? And he'll tell me. And I might pick something up that way.

> You watch how other people do the job and you learn from that. Or they might have a different approach to you or a different perspective on a certain problem. (All quotes from Billett 1994b.)

The contributions the physical environment makes to learning are not always fully acknowledged. As with the barmaid's example, this kind of learning is usually associated with visual clues for how tasks are to be completed and other clues and cues provided by the workplace itself. A warehouse worker referred to the 'library' of pallet-packing combinations available in the warehouse in which she worked (Billett 1993b). Whenever faced with a new box shape or uncertainty about how to pack a pallet, she was able to refer to the library of examples that were all around her. Lave's (1990) tailors used half-completed garments as means to gauge the quality of their own work. In these ways, models, cues and clues about how to proceed are available in workplaces. Both indirect interactions with others and the physical workplace environment are particularly useful as sources of goals and sub-goals for workplace tasks, and also as a means for observing and learning workplace procedures.

In summary, the key contributions to learning in the workplace are located in engagement in activities, and in the direct and indirect guidance accessed in the workplace. The quality of learning in workplaces is therefore premised on the availability of access to routine and non-routine activities that will assist individuals to learn new knowledge and develop that knowledge further through practice and guidance. Much of this is provided freely in workplaces; however, it is difficult to simulate or reproduce these kinds of guidance or authentic workplace experiences elsewhere. For example, the shift of nurse preparation from hospitals to universities has been accompanied by concerns about the lack of authentic workplace practice required for nursing expertise. One solution has been to build mock hospital wards in universities and provide students with access to simulated activities in these environments. However, is it not clear how useful it is create a substitute workplace environment. As one experienced nurse stated: 'Do these wards have staff who squabble, interns who are working 70 hours a week, orderlies who are either helpful or reluctant to help? Do these wards have "golden staph" [staphylococcus aureus—an antibiotic-resistant bacterium] and do they have patients that wake up at three in the morning and paint "poo" on the walls?' As this nurse suggests, workplaces are more than physical environments. They are social systems, and workplace activities are premised on interactions with others and artefacts as components of a particular work practice. Moreover, the contributions of indirect guidance are ongoing in these work practices. Individuals are immersed in workplace activities and interactions, making these contributions to learning almost unavoidable. Such activities and guidance are central to the moment-by-moment learning that we participate in as we think and act every day. It is these kinds of contributions that are provided freely in the workplace and that also need to be accentuated as opportunities to derive rich learning. However, other contributions are also provided freely as part of everyday activities in the workplace. Some of these are associated with the learning of knowledge that is either inappropriate or not likely to assist developing expertise. These shortcomings need to be considered alongside other evidence of the limitations of learning in workplaces.

LIMITATIONS OF WORKPLACES AS LEARNING ENVIRONMENTS

> The trouble with learning on-the-job . . . you're only as good as the situations you come up . . . and the people you are working with and their ability to communicate. (Quoted in Billett 1994b.)

There are a number of limitations associated with learning in the workplace that were identified in the workplace studies referred to at the beginning of this chapter. The limitations are associated with either inappropriate contributions or gaps in the requirements to develop expertise in the workplace. It is important to understand these limitations in order that workplace learning arrangements, such as a workplace curriculum, can attempt to address or marginalise these shortcomings. From the findings of the workplace learning studies, learning in the workplace can be weakened by: (a) learning that is inappropriate, yet available in the workplace; (b) learning that flounders because the contested nature of participation in work practice inhibits individuals' access to activities and guidance; (c) the difficulty of learning knowledge that is not readily accessible in the workplace; (d) difficulty associated with accessing appropriate expertise and experiences required to develop vocational practice; and (e) the reluctance of workers to participate in learning vocational practice that is available through workplace experiences (Billett 1993a, 1993b, 1994a, 1994b, 1996b; Billett et al. 1998; Billett & Rose 1999).

Learning inappropriate knowledge

You do not always get an overall view of the job.

You are probably shown the quickest way to do the job, but not the correct way. They show you the shortcuts. (Quotes from Billett 1994b.)

Because learning is a product of everyday thinking and acting, it is inevitable that not all learning will be desirable or appropriate. Learning that might be considered undesirable and inappropriate is not quarantined in some way in the workplace. Some of these outcomes are likely to be associated with unsafe working practices, or with the failure to use the requisite amount of checking and monitoring required for work tasks. In addition, there may be work practices that encourage exclusiveness and intolerance in the workplace. Inappropriate knowledge, including attitudes and values (e.g. dangerous work practice or exclusive views about gender/race), might well be learnt if it is practised and/or rewarded in the workplace (Harris & Volet 1996, 1997). Inappropriate learning outcomes can arise from incomplete preparation. Through their everyday work activities, production workers in the electronics industry had learnt to use diagnostic software quite inefficiently (Darrah 1997). Because these workers did not understand how to operate the software, they believed it had to work through an entire diagnostic cycle each time, rather than being programmed for the much shorter and focused cycles required for particular diagnostic tasks (Darrah 1996). For these production workers, because the 'process of learning is largely by imitation and because many of the trainers are uncertified, bad practices can spread quickly' (Darrah 1996: 19). Unsafe work practices can also be learnt through workplace learning provisions (Harris et al. 1996b).

However, there may be different views about what constitutes appropriate learning, just as there might be quite different perspectives about performance. This applies as much to learning associated with values and attitudes as to the concepts and procedures required for work. Through their everyday participation, coal workers experience the ongoing contestation between workers and management which is very much a part of the culture of coal mining (Billett 1993a,

1995b). In doing so, they are more or less likely to construct a particular set of values about coal mining, whereas supervisors will construct a different set. Equally, both sets of workers will develop different sets of practices and strategies designed to combat each other's goals. Whether or not these learning outcomes can be described as 'inappropriate' depends on one's views about the merits of such contestation, and in whose interests they should be resolved—that is what constitutes appropriate learning. It has been shown that, on leaving the police academy and participating in routine police work, novice officers have been told by more experienced officers to forget what they have learnt in the academy. Consequently, novice police officers may ignore their training because of peer pressure. This has been claimed to result in the violation of civil rights by these officers (Independent Commission on the Los Angeles Police Department 1991, cited in Anderson et al. 1996). Therefore, the values embedded in workplaces and what is modelled there are likely to play a role in determining what workers learn and hence how they perform. The kinds of practices emphasised and rewarded, and the behaviour that is de-emphasised—the culture of work practice (Brown et al. 1989)—will likely influence learning through engagement in the workplace.

It should not be assumed, however, that learning bad work practices is inevitable. Individuals determine what they learn from a situation by whether they wish to identify with what they experience (Hodges 1998). Although associated with identity formation with the particular practice (Lave & Wenger 1991), learning through participation is not 'socialisation' or mere 'internalisation'. Individuals do not mindlessly learn the attitudes, values and identity associated with work practice. Nor do they necessarily conform to the practice (Hodges 1998). However, the dominant values of the workplace may be influential, particularly in what novices learn at work. This includes their attitudes and values, as they try to participate and find acceptance in the workplace. For instance, it would be difficult for new production workers in coal mines to be able to openly demonstrate agreement with management policies or for novice police officers to violate the culture of police practice set down by their colleagues without being ostracised for holding such views and taking these actions. Such conditions are not restricted to coal mines or police work. Workplaces inevitably have a culture of work practice that affords and privileges knowledge in particular ways. Harris et al. (1996a) also note there is sometimes confusion about what constitutes the 'right way' in workplaces. For instance, each shift of a food processing plant believes that it knows the optimum way of operating the plant. If individuals learn that there is just 'one way' of performing tasks, this might inhibit transfer to other tasks and situations. This concern was evident in the hairdressing study, where one owner was quite insistent that his approach to hairdressing was superior to others, and particularly to what was taught in vocational colleges. He insisted that his approaches and techniques had to be used in the salon (Billett 1995a). However, his apprentices ultimately had the opportunity to attend college and learn different approaches, and also to learn from other apprentices about how hairdressing was undertaken in other salons. So learning will take place that is unintended. It could be even be detrimental to the development of expertise or contrary to safe routine performance. Just as with learning in educational institutions, there are unintended outcomes (a 'hidden curriculum') in workplaces. However, although the concern about learning inappropriate knowledge is important and needs to be addressed, it would be wrong to assume that this problem relates only to workplaces. Instead, it reflects concerns about learning in the both the classroom *and* the workplace. Nevertheless, a clear limitation for workplace learning is that individuals learn unintended knowledge as well as outcomes that are undesirable because they comprise short cuts, bad habits or even dangerous practice. This limitation needs to be considered in workplace-based arrangements.

Access to workplace activities

Two sets of concerns have been identified that are associated with the ability of learners to engage in the kinds of activities required for developing expertise in the workplace. Firstly, being able to undertake a combination of routine and non-routine workplace activities is necessary in order to learn and reinforce vocational knowledge. Secondly, as workplaces are often contested environments, learners may have difficulty gaining access to opportunities and tasks because access is quite deliberately being inhibited. Taking the first of these points, the quantity and quality of guided access to authentic workplace activities is going to be a key determinant for developing vocational expertise. The earlier nursing example emphasised the need to access activities that are authentic, in terms of how those activities will be enacted. Collectively, these contributions are what has been referred to as *distributed cognition* (Hutchins 1991; Pea 1993; Resnick et al. 1997)—the requirements to learn and perform are distributed across the work practice. Without being able to access authentic experiences and understand the requirements for performance, it is unlikely that learners will develop the abilities necessary for expert performance. Access to routine as well as non-routine work activities is vital for developing the kinds of procedures required for effective work performance, as detailed in Chapter 2. For instance, through witnessing many births, midwives build up a rich repertoire of signs and indications about births as well as the scope for different types of births. These experiences are contrasted with those reported of specialists who attend only difficult births (Billett 1999b). Consequently, midwives claim to have developed a far greater understanding of birthing mothers' conditions. These understandings are premised on indicators such as the sheen of the birthing mother's skin and the avoidance of eye contact at certain times in the birthing process. Further, because midwives experience a wide range of birth types, they develop a rich understanding of different birthing scenarios that aids the diagnosis of birthing (Billett 1999b). All of these need to be learnt through authentic engagement in work.

Therefore, if learners are denied engagement in activities—particularly those of a non-routine nature—learning outcomes may be limited, as they may fail to develop rich procedures. Conversely, learners may be asked to complete tasks that are beyond what they can reasonably achieve without close guidance. The lack of readiness could result in levels of disequilibrium and anxiety resulting in confusion and a reluctance to engage further in the task. Ask any teacher about the time(s) that they almost lost control of a class and the impact it had on their approach to teaching. However, the readiness to participate is likely to be quite person-dependent. For example, a worker with low-level work skills or low literacy levels may find it too difficult to complete tasks that others could perform with ease. In addition, unless access to work activities is sequenced to take the novice from engaging in peripheral activities through to increasingly accountable and varying types of tasks (Harris et al. 1996a), there could be limited outcomes for learners (Moore 1986). Consequently, a workplace curriculum needs to secure access to combinations of routine and non-routine experiences that constitute a pathway towards expertise.

Understanding the goals for workplace performance

Learners also need to be able to visualise and understand the desired outcomes of their work in order to develop goals for performance. At least two levels of goals need to be made explicit: goals associated with overall task completion, and sub-goals of the particular tasks in which they are engaged. In one investigation, the pallet-packers in a warehouse accompanied the delivery truck to a supermarket. This activity was organised to develop an appreciation of what happens to the pallet in transit and at the unloading bay at the supermarket. This was used to develop an understanding about the requirements of pallet packing in order for the stock to arrive at the supermarket in a saleable condition (Billett 1993b, 1994a). These are important understandings. If these workers had been denied the opportunity to learn these important work performance goals, they might have found it difficult to understand the requirements for their work. Significantly, in the coal mining industry, workers at the coal processing part of the production process complained about too much foreign material coming from the mine (Billett 1995b). However, few of the coal miners had ever visited this plant or understood the processes it used or the impact of foreign material on its operation and on the quality of the coal. Barriers to broader access to work tasks, such as the demarcations in some coal mines, may make it more difficult for these workers to understand the requirements of related work processes. Consequently, if combinations of activities that workers are allowed to participate in are restricted, the scope and depth of their knowledge, including goals for performance and the kinds of knowledge they can construct, could be limited.

Further, learners' access to workplace activities and goals will not always be facilitated. Learning often occurs in circumstances where relationships between participants are unequal (Verodonik et al. 1988) and workplaces are no exception to this (Moore 1986; Billett 1999a). Sometimes work practice is structured in ways that inhibit the very access that would assist the understanding of workplace goals. For instance, in the coal mining industry, seniority is sometimes used to determine opportunities to access new kinds of experiences. Premised on the rule of 'first on, last off', opportunities for development are made available depending on employees' length of service or seniority. This can frustrate the new employee who is keen to progress. In other circumstances, access to activities is based on the status of employment (Darrah 1997) or the language skills of the worker (Hull 1997). Darrah (1997) notes how the system designers were the 'heroes' in a computer manufacturing company. The production workers, although engaged in highly complex work, did not receive the acknowledgment, support or standing that their work warranted. The provision of support and acknowledgment in this workplace was distributed asymmetrically, premised on perceptions of the standing of the work being done. Equally, there is a wealth of research indicating that women are often excluded intentionally from participation in workplaces (e.g. Butler 1999; Probert 1999). So it cannot be assumed that mere participation in the workplace will deliver equity of access to the kinds of activities required for developing performance for the workplace. Therefore, it is necessary to account for how workplaces can furnish access to combinations of routine and non-routine experiences for learners, as well as for how activities can be structured for the goals and sub-goals required for successful work performance. These concerns have led to consideration of the 'learning curriculum' (Lave 1990), which is conceptualised here to include an ordering of learners' access to these kinds of experiences. It is proposed that experiences in the workplace be structured and sequenced to provide a pathway of both routine and non-routine activities to take learners from peripheral to full participation, accessing the goals for performance while part of the pathway (Billett 1996b, 1996c).

Reluctance of experts to provide guidance

Consistent with concerns about both contestation in the workplace and the quality of guidance is the need for learners to work collaboratively with experts in the workplace. Experts' reluctance to guide and provide close interactions will likely weaken the quality of workplace learning. Such reluctance may arise from fears about loss of status (Moore 1986) or concerns about being displaced by those whom they have guided and supported (Lave & Wenger 1991). In Japanese corporations, where workplace learning is institutionalised, supervisors routinely develop the skills of their subordinates (Dore & Sako 1989). Because promotion is based on seniority in these corporations, supervisors are secure from being replaced or displaced by those whose learning they have guided. However, this may not be the case in other countries. Experts who fear displacement by those whom they assist to learn may, understandably, be unwilling to provide close guidance or access to increasingly accountable tasks. So, whereas for the teacher the sharing of knowledge is a given, this may not be the case for more experienced coworkers in workplaces.

In an investigation of guided learning in five workplaces (Billett et al. 1998), some of the workers selected as mentors in one enterprise were suspicious of management's motivation in nominating them for this role. Hence their interactions with the learners were hesitant and infrequent in some instances. The evidence of learning outcomes was lower in this enterprise than for other enterprises where interactions were more positively grounded and frequent. Yet, even in this environment, one mentor was highly active and assisted his assigned learners (see Table 3.2, subjects E23/24). The reported outcomes for these learners were distinctly more positive than for others in this enterprise. The learners themselves reported the contributions of their mentor most positively, and the development of their own self-worth arising out of an opportunity to learn more about their work (Billett et al. 1998). This finding illustrates differences in outcomes premised on the reluctance or enthusiasm of more experienced coworkers acting as guides.

A particular issue for guidance by more experienced workers in some workplaces is concern about industrial or professional affiliations (i.e. demarcations) (Owen 1995, 1999). This can influence interactions between workers, as well as restrict access to workplace expertise. For example, tradespersons may be reluctant to assist a non-tradesperson with a particular task if they believe it may jeopardise their own interests or those with whom they are affiliated (e.g. union). The same is likely to be true of the professions as well. However, the same tradesperson might work conscientiously with an apprentice who is correctly affiliated. In the coal mines, there is a practice of the quarantining of skills by particular industrial (union) affiliations. This demarcation is central to the organisation and distribution of work in the mines. In these workplaces, although guidance was available for novices, it was confined to particular streams of work activity (Billett 1995b). However, even within the formal demarcations in the coal mines, there are historical alliances between groups that have sought to further demarcate access to work activities. Workers who were historically associated with particular pieces of equipment (through previously separate union affiliation) were given preference when it came to access to equipment and guidance in its use (Billett 1995b).

In the secondary processing plant, there was no official demarcation based on skills. Non-tradeworkers conducted the trade-type tasks they were competent to perform, whereas tradeworkers undertook production tasks that would, in other workplaces, have been restricted to trade assistants. However, despite there being no official demarcation in this workplace, engineers' views were held to be superordinate to those of the production workers, despite the latter group's often deep knowledge of and intimacy with the production plant (Billett 1994b). This left the production workers feeling frustrated and disempowered. Both of these situations focus on issues of access to guidance by experts. In the coal mines, a more experienced coworker would be reluctant to provide guidance to learners if a task was outside their demarcated area of work. Equally, the engineer in the secondary processing plant may not be willing to share knowledge with production workers for similar reasons. Finally, more than just gaining access to experts, the quality of interactions between expert and learner is also important. If the expert merely tells, rather than modelling, demonstrating and working collaboratively with the learner, the outcomes might be quite weak (Harris et al. 1996a). These researchers also raise concerns about experts' expectations being unrealistic, because they fail to understand how long it takes to become competent in particular activities. So reluctance on the part of experts to understand learners' needs and a desire to teach rather than guide will restrict the quality of learning outcomes. Ideally, learners need interactions with more experienced colleagues who are enthusiastic, supportive, well focused and can engage learners in thinking for themselves. All this suggests a need for preparation for workplace guides, and considerations for their practice that include the quality of relations between experienced coworkers and learners in the workplace.

Absence of expert guidance

Learning on the job in isolation just takes a long time.

Not knowing, no support, no guidelines—it has just been a process of trial and error. (Quotes from Billett 1994b.)

The absence of experts to provide guidance is likely to inhibit the quality of workplace learning (Moore 1986; Billett 1994b, 1994c). In some circumstances, there will be no expertise in the workplace. This is likely to be the case when there has been significant change to either the kinds of work being undertaken or the requirements for performance. An example of the former might be when new technology arrives or where new work practices and goals transform the work previously undertaken. For example, many publicly funded schools and kindergartens have suddenly become wholly responsible for their own budgets. The principal's role has changed from that of educational administrator and leader to business manager. Another example is when the learner is physically or geographically remote from expert guidance. In both these instances, expertise may simply be unavailable in the workplace. The transfer of knowledge may be quite limited if there are new tasks that require knowledge not accessible in the workplace.

Also, learners' views about who is capable of providing expert guidance are important. In the coal mining study (Billett 1993a), it was claimed that the teachers at a nearby vocational college lacked appropriate expertise in how work was conducted in the mines. Hence the miners perceived these teachers as being unable to provide the kind of guidance required in the coal mines. This was the case even with vocational activities that were not peculiar to coal mines, such as diesel fitting. Instead, the miners reported relying on expertise available in the coal mines and through vendor training provided by equipment manufacturers. This was one of the few situations when expertise external to the coal mining community was really valued. However, even here the miners were selective about what they regarded as credible sources of advice. With the vendor training, they valued only the advice and guidance provided by the vendor trainers on how the equipment operated (e.g. mechanical, electronic and hydraulic systems). The miners claimed to know more about how to use the equipment than the vendor trainers. The significance of appraisals of the legitimacy of the expert is that it is the workplace learner who determines who is a credible source of knowledge (Billett 1994; Volkoff 1996). Although somebody might be nominated as a trainer or mentor in an enterprise, it is the learners who ultimately determine whether they are a credible source of knowledge. They are the meaning makers who decide what they learn and value. As these instances illustrate, the presence of expertise and views about the legitimacy of that expertise are important for the quality of guided learning in workplaces. An absence of expertise can limit access to knowledge that will not be learnt by discovery alone. The expert's standing as a source of credible learning will also be determined by those in the workplace.

Developing understanding in the workplace

They show you the shortcuts . . . not knowing why you're doing what you've been told to do—for instance changing a diverter: why are you diverting material and where to?

Didn't understand what the job was all about—I just done a job.

Not broad-based learning; skills targeted to job at hand only. [On the job training was not useful when] attempting to deal with unusual situations.

Did not provide an overall understanding of material. (All quotes from Billett 1994b.)

In all the studies, concerns arose about the development of understanding by workplace learners. There was consistent evidence that the requisite levels of understanding required for work practice were not being achieved through everyday engagement in work. In two investigations (Billett 1993b, 1994b), workers reported the inability of everyday activities in the workplace to secure the depth of understanding required for their work activities. In another, it was clear that conceptual development was uneven, being dependent on what was or was not discussed in the workplace (Billett 1995a). This is a concern that deserves particular consideration, given the importance of the understanding required for effective vocational practice. Firstly, much conceptual knowledge is 'hidden' from everyday workplace activity. Workers' ability to understand factors such as force, hygiene, voltage, physiology and so on may not readily be learnt through workplace activity. Consequently, this knowledge may need to be made transparent and accessible to learners through expert guidance or some other strategy. The second concern is that everyday experiences in the workplace may result in understanding that is piecemeal rather than being comprehensive enough to respond to new tasks. Workers referred to having learnt tasks, but did not always understand why they were doing them or the consequences of what they were doing (Billett 1994b). At the secondary processing plant, some of these respondents suggested that 'theory' should be included in workplace learning experiences because of their concern about a lack of understanding.

In the hairdressing study, the development of conceptual knowledge was influenced by the degree to which the knowledge to be learnt was accessible in the workplace. However, not all concepts associated with hairdressing were discussed in the workplace (e.g. hair structure). Those concepts frequently discussed were found to develop in a more uniform and richly interlinked way. However, concepts that were opaque and not the subject of discussion in the workplace (e.g. hair structure) were represented in quite idiosyncratic ways by learners (Billett 1995a). It seems that, on their own, everyday work activities cannot provide the understanding required for expertise at work. Prawat (1993) and Evans (1993) suggest that situated learning, such as that in the workplace, may favour the development of procedural knowledge and ignore conceptual development. Gott (1995) also questions the efficacy of current approaches to apprenticeship learning in securing the conceptual knowledge required for 'high-tech' tasks. Studies of CNC lathe operators (Martin & Scribner 1991) and process workers (Zuboff 1988) emphasise how the separation of the worker from direct contact with the equipment they operate and the symbolic requirements for its operation make the knowledge to be learnt more conceptual and more difficult to learn. Significantly, as Berryman (1993) argues, this type of knowledge is increasingly required for workplace performance in technology-driven workplaces and those with complex organisational and task-structuring activities.

A concern is that participation in work tasks alone may lead to understanding that is disconnected rather than richly associated. There are ways of avoiding this outcome. For example, with nurse education in major teaching hospitals, the novice nurses are rotated through different wards, thereby systematically providing experiences about nursing in different contexts. These preparatory experiences might involve nurses working in the casualty section, wards dealing with general care, specialised care, intensive care, nursing those patients who are permanently incapacitated, those who are dying, those who are giving or have given birth and those who have mental health problems. This structuring of experiences helps develop understanding about important concepts of nursing. It embeds the individuals' nursing concepts and procedures in a range of practices that then assist their transfer to other nursing situations. Despite the concerns expressed above, some forms of conceptual knowledge are developed through guided everyday activities in the workplace (Billett 1994b; Billett & Rose 1999). It is erroneous to suggest that procedures are privileged in workplaces and concepts in the schoolroom, as Evans (1993) and Prawat (1993) warn. However, given the importance of understanding to vocational expertise, and the importance of developing richly associated conceptual knowledge, it is appropriate to place a particular emphasis on its coherent development in workplace settings. Guided learning by more experienced coworkers will probably be required to generate understanding within the constraints of the workplace activities. For the development of understanding, the structuring of experiences, close guidance and/or instructional interventions may serve to access and develop knowledge that is opaque and hidden from the novices. In particular, the selected use of strategies that aim to develop conceptual knowledge in the workplace is warranted. These are discussed in Chapter 5.

Reluctance of workers to participate

It is important to acknowledge that not all workers are willing participants in the learning process. Given the central role of the individual in constructing their knowledge, their reluctance to engage is of particular concern. The refusal to engage purposefully in goal-directed activities and interact with more experienced workers will likely result in weak learning. Therefore, it is necessary to consider how this reluctance can be overcome and to engage learners in the demanding process of learning new knowledge. Examples of reluctance to participate were evident in workplace investigations, particularly where there was a structured training program. The reluctance of two workers to engage with the formalised program because of their literacy skills was evident in their low level of participation (Billett 1994b). Others were concerned about potential embarrassment associated with low performance with assessment tasks located in text-based materials. Sources of reluctance can also be cultural. Coal miners reported being suspicious of safety training programs which were perceived as merely a means to pass the responsibility and liability for safety on to workers (Billett 1995b). In one enterprise (Billett et al. 1998), a mentor had difficulty working with a new employee who saw himself as being at least as capable as the mentor. Also, the new employee had a set of values quite distinct from those adopted in the workplace, and was reluctant to accept the values of his new workplace. Given this kind of reluctance, engagement is unlikely to result in learning the requirements for effective work performance. Such resistance was also evident in the case of the Vietnamese workers in the computer manufacturing plant mentioned earlier. These workers were reluctant to engage in team-based work. Darrah (1996: 27) states: 'One supervisor's explanation that diverse members were to work together "at the same level" only exacerbated their belief that communism had indeed followed them to the United States.'

However, reluctance or disinterest is a common—perhaps *the* most common—experience of participation in educational programs. It is more than a lack of attention—it threatens the quality of learning. There will always be differences between individuals' values and priorities and what is emphasised in any social practice, particularly in the workplace. In some instances this is quite healthy and constructive, as critical challenges can lead to renewal and the forging of a new direction. Yet there will be other circumstances where a reluctance to participate will result in weak learning outcomes in important areas of vocational practice. The development and deployment of higher order procedures and forming associations between various units of conceptual knowledge are likely to require effort on the part of the learners and some guidance by experts. Hence a workplace curriculum needs to find ways of encouraging willing and committed participation by those in the workplace. This includes attempting to overcome hesitancy associated with concerns about performance abilities or potential embarrassment. Ways of addressing cultural inhibitors and engaging individuals therefore arise as key challenges for workplace learning.

SUMMARY

This chapter has identified and discussed the inherent contributions and potential weaknesses of learning in workplaces. Many contributions to learning are provided freely by the workplace and workers engage in learning processes as part of everyday work activities. However, some of the limitations are so inherent to work practice (e.g. demarcation, distrust, isolation, absence of experts) that they are difficult to overcome and may resist and frustrate easy solutions. However, the identification of the contribution the workplace provides in the form of activities and guidance, together with a clearer understanding of the factors that may inhibit the development of expertise at work, provides a basis for constructing a workplace curriculum. Overcoming or inhibiting the weaknesses identified above informs the kinds of interventions that will be required as components of the workplace curriculum. Arrangements to overcome or inhibit these concerns include: (a) making accessible knowledge that might not be learnt alone; (b) determining a pathway of activities; and (c) providing close guidance to develop appropriate procedures and insights. Collectively, these can be thought of as the basis for a learning curriculum for the workplace (Lave 1990; Billett 1996b).

The qualities of the activities in which individuals engage in the workplace and the guidance they receive influence what they learn about their vocational practice. The quality of these experiences and interactions is structured by the norms and values of the workplace and the willingness of experts or experienced others to assist other workers to learn. However, the workers will not learn a set body of knowledge about the vocation (if such a thing actually exists). Instead, the types of activities that occur in the workplace ('what we do here is . . .') and the way that work is undertaken ('how we do things here is . . .') influence what is learnt. However, there is also a 'hidden curriculum' of workplaces. Unintended learning results from engaging in workplace activities, and some of these unintended outcomes may be undesirable in terms of the development of expertise. Short-cuts, dangerous work practices, inappropriate behaviours, the reinforcement of restrictive practices such as non-inclusive behaviour and problems associated with the development of understanding have been identified as limitations associated with learning in the workplace as part of everyday work activities. The key goal for a workplace curriculum is to develop the knowledge required for expert performance. This requirement refers to more than the acquisition of 'technical skills'. It extends to the capacity to think and act in ways that permit individuals to resolve non-routine problems, to understand what constitutes an appropriate action and to become a full participant whose contributions are such that they themselves shape work practice in particular ways. The knowledge required for expertise is most likely acquired through a combination of engagement in work tasks of increasing accountability, the close guidance of other workers and experts, and the more indirect ongoing guidance provided by the setting. As individuals use their knowledge at work, procedures are being tested, modified and reinforced through interactions with workplace tasks. Engagement in everyday work also provides opportunities to develop expertise through observation, to generate tentative solutions to workplace tasks and then to seek to secure those solutions—a process directly or indirectly guided by more experienced coworkers. However, such experiences and guidance will not occur without some interventions: organisation, maintenance and the use of selected strategies for guided learning.

Taken together, the kinds of contributions identified here are those that will be used in Part II of this book, which presents the structure of a curriculum for the workplace.

PART II

Guided learning at work: A curriculum for the workplace

4

A workplace curriculum model

A CURRICULUM FOR THE WORKPLACE

There is clear evidence that workers learn through everyday activities in the workplace. So why is it necessary to attempt to organise and structure further workplace experiences? The previous chapters have shown that it is important to both maximise what is provided freely through these experiences and augment them by interventions that extend those contributions while inhibiting or curtailing factors that obstruct the development of vocational expertise. It is as vital for individuals to realise their vocational goals as it is for enterprises to have workers able to adapt to the changing requirements of their work practice. Accordingly, this chapter describes a curriculum model for the workplace and proposes how it would be developed. Ideas advanced in earlier chapters about the strengths and weaknesses of learning in workplaces and the kinds of learning required for effective performance at work are drawn upon and expanded.

This curriculum model seeks to make full use of the learning available through everyday participation in work activities guided by expert coworkers and assisted by the contributions of other workers and the workplace environment itself. Together, these contributions have the potential to provide kinds of learning experiences that are unavailable elsewhere. These principles remain the core elements of this model of curriculum and an accompanying pedagogy for the workplace. They are founded on investigations into learning for and in workplaces. There is coincidence between these concerns and the goals that enterprises seek from work-based learning experiences. Enterprises need to consider structuring workplace learning experiences as suggested in the workplace curriculum, in order to address many of their requirements for work-based learning. Without this structuring, the full potential of learning experiences in the workplace will not be realised. Consequently, the workplace curriculum model is intended to assist workers wishing to learn about or develop further their vocational knowledge and to help enterprises organise effective workplace learning. In addition, it can also be used to enrich vocational education programs that are shared between the workplace and an educational institution. The principles underpinning this model are intended to:

- provide structured experiences to develop in individuals the attributes required for expert work performance;
- identify and structure a pathway of learning experiences that take into account enterprise needs and those of the individuals who are learning;
- use direct guidance to assist the development of understandings and hone procedures required for expert practice;
- assist learners to participate fully through structured learning arrangements that provide access to indirect guidance in the workplace; and
- focus on a learning curriculum, rather than one in which direct teaching predominates.

A MODEL OF A WORKPLACE CURRICULUM

The model of a workplace curriculum proposed here is based on the structuring of activities and guidance in the workplace—on guided learning at work. The model proposes organising access to a pathway of activities which takes a learner from being a novice through to being an expert in the work practice—from peripheral to full participation (Lave & Wenger 1991). The pathway engages learners in movement from work activities of low accountability and complexity to activities that are high in accountability and complexity. For individual workers, the guidance assists with identifying and understanding workplace goals, accessing knowledge that is hard to learn alone and progressing along the pathway of work activities. The curriculum comes into effect as workers engage in the ordinary activities of the workplace. It is explicitly structured to take maximum advantage of opportunities provided freely in the workplace, while also attempting to address some of the limitations of workplace learning experiences in developing expert performance at work. From this, it is proposed that the four key elements in the structuring of a workplace curriculum are:

- movement from participation in low- to high-accountability work activities;
- access to knowledge that would not be learnt by discovery alone;
- direct guidance from more experienced others and experts; and
- indirect guidance provided by the physical and social environment.

These elements of the workplace curriculum are described below and depicted in Figure 4.1. This figure illustrates the pathway of activities in which individuals will engage as they move from novice to expert participation. In the sections that follow, each of the elements of the workplace curriculum is explained and illustrated. Principles associated with organising these experiences in the workplace are also identified within each section.

Movement from peripheral to full participation

In order to structure experiences for learners to acquire the knowledge required for performance at work, it is necessary to identify a pathway of activities that leads from peripheral to full participation in the workplace. This structuring is based on the pathway that

Figure 4.1 A model of workplace curriculum

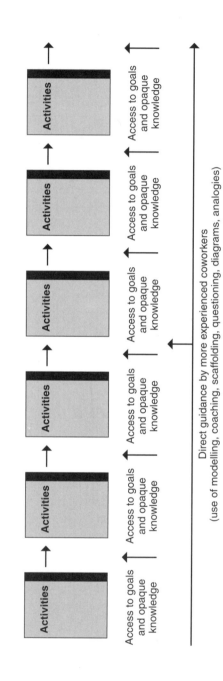

Movement from peripheral to full participation in the work practice

Peripheral participation
(Activities of low accountability and low complexity)

Full participation
(Activities of high accountability, high complexity)

Indirect guidance
(Contributions of the workplace setting and through observation and listening)

Activities

Access to goals and opaque knowledge

Direct guidance by more experienced coworkers
(use of modelling, coaching, scaffolding, questioning, diagrams, analogies)

would be undertaken by novices on their way to becoming experts in the workplace, founded on their movement from activities that are less accountable and complex to those which are more complex and carry greater accountability (see Figure 4.1). In Lave's (1990) study, the tailors' apprentices commenced by ironing completed garments, going on to engage in finishing activities (sewing hems and buttons).

The first garments the apprentices produced themselves were those of lower levels of accountability—children's underwear, then adults' underwear, then children's clothes such as pants and shirts, before going on to manufacture adult shirts. If mistakes were made with these garments, the consequences would be limited. Later, when the apprentices became much more proficient, they were able to learn to manufacture high-status ceremonial garments worn at important social events. These garments required high levels of skills. Because they were made of expensive cloth, mistakes could not easily be tolerated. In a similar way, hairdressing apprentices initially engaged in 'tea and tidy' activities before being permitted to wash and rinse clients' hair. Next they assisted senior hairdressers and were only able to cut women's hair in some salons after considerable practice on males.

The sequencing of workplace activities assists learners to engage in incrementally more complex tasks and goals in the movement from being novices to experts in the workplace.

> Board techs are trained through gradual exposure to increasingly complex PCBs. A lead technician . . . assigns new workers to the automatic testing machine for a few weeks so they learn the characteristics of the individual tests, their sequence, and typical error messages. Then he allows them to trouble shoot simpler PCBs, such as memory or input output boards. After three or four months, technicians are able to recognise error messages and pinpoint the defective areas of the boards. Gradually, they tackle the more complex PCBs. (Darrah 1996: 18)

This sequencing of access to workplace tasks has a particular and deliberate purpose. With the tailors' apprentices, the ironing of garments permitted the novices to become familiar with completed garments. The sequence permits an understanding of the overall requirements for making the garments, before considering the requirements of particular procedures—from the global to the local (Collins et al. 1989), thereby enacting an important principle about how learning might best proceed. The ironing of completed garments permits the identification of the garments' component parts, the shape of these parts and the standard of finish required. The same goes for the finishing off of garments. The manufacture of whole garments, such as children's underclothes, was useful in understanding the construction of a complete garment and how it should be assembled, seaming and the sequencing of assembly. In a similar way, the hairdressing apprentices learnt about the needs for tidiness and hygiene through their 'tea and tidy' activities. In undertaking these tasks, they also learnt how to communicate with customers—something they developed further when engaged in washing and rinsing customers' hair.

The structuring of these experiences is premised on engagement in movement from tasks of low to high accountability and complexity. However, this structuring provides—albeit implicitly—important foundational knowledge of the vocational practice. This includes an understanding of the overall goals for work (e.g. the required finish of a garment or haircut) and sub-goals associated with work practice (e.g. keeping the salon clean and tidy, the accuracy required when seaming garments, sequence in seaming garments). This represents an important pedagogical principle and basis for instructional design for the workplace. However, unless the requirements of practice demand it, the pathway of experiences does not have to be a fixed sequence of activities undertaken in a lockstep fashion. Instead, a group of activities can be identified which can be accessed and undertaken by learners as opportunities arise and the learners' readiness dictates. The ongoing consideration of how learning could be realised through opportunities provided by work activities could assist the structuring of these experiences. In Japanese corporations, the practice is for supervisors to ensure that all subordinates are provided with opportunities to learn about their work (Dore & Sako 1989). Therefore, when a work task has to be undertaken, the supervisor may consider which staff member will benefit most from being involved in undertaking the task or being able to observe its completion.

Progress along the pathway needs also to be premised on learners' ability—their 'readiness'—to commence the tasks either independently or with the guidance of a more experienced coworker. Movement along such a pathway is not restricted to novices. It can also be used for experienced workers moving into new work areas. Indeed, it may be possible to identify points where the pathways of experiences coincide with those of a new or different work area. For instance, where workers are being multi-skilled, they are likely to encounter activities that represent a clear departure from what they already know and do. However, movement along such a pathway may be made difficult by divisions of labour in workplaces that truncate and/or inhibit this movement (Lave 1991).

The first component of the workplace curriculum is thus the identification and establishment of a pathway or pathways of work activities to organise and structure the experiences of learners, so they may participate more fully in the workplace. Principles for this component of the workplace curriculum are as follows:

In terms of activities:

- movement from less to more complex tasks;
- movement from the global to the local;
- movement from less to more accountable tasks;
- provision of access to experiences that build up knowledge by understanding the goals and procedures required for performance.

In terms of guidance:

- activities that are structured in such a way as to accommodate learners' incremental and structured development;
- access to modelling and procedures that are observable and thereby provide important foundations for learning and performance;
- movement through activities linked to learners' 'readiness'.

Access to goals for performance and knowledge that are difficult to learn

Learners' workplace experiences need to include opportunities to understand the requirements for work performance—goals for the work tasks. Without this understanding, workers cannot effectively direct their activities towards achieving these goals. Also, as learning is through engagement in workplace activities, the quality of desired outcomes and the energies to be directed towards achieving those goals will be linked to understanding what is to be learnt. If individuals are unaware of the importance of a particular task, they may not expend the effort required to learn to perform that task to the required level. Consequently, the pathway of experiences has to afford opportunities to access both the requirements for (goals) and the means for undertaking (procedures) workplace activities (see Figure 4.1).

Through participation in workplace activities, indirect guidance is available. Observation of other workers and models provided for the conduct of work provides this form of guidance. Office workers reported that opportunities to observe how more experienced colleagues dealt with different kinds of customers were highly instructive (Billett 1993b). In the hairdressing salons, the practice of looking at completed hair treatments provides apprentices with access to models of and goals for performance. This was also evident in Lave's (1990) tailoring examples, which involved apprentices finishing and ironing garments. The opportunity to observe and comprehend the requirements for performance assists in developing an understanding of what approaches or orientations are likely to be successful in particular circumstances.

However, access to understanding the requirements for performance is not always explicitly available. Consequently, it may be necessary to structure experiences to provide access to work performance goals that might otherwise not be learnt. As noted earlier, warehouse workers accompanied delivery trucks to supermarkets to witness the delivery of the goods they had packed on to pallets (Billett 1993b). This experience allowed these workers to appreciate the care and thoroughness required in packing the pallets to withstand the rigours of long road journeys and unloading procedures at supermarkets. The structuring of this experience was a direct means of assisting the warehouse workers to understand requirements for work performance which would otherwise remain unknown to them. In the secondary processing plant (Billett 1994b), production employees assigned to light duties because of workplace injuries often worked in the laboratory that monitored the quality of the plant's products. These workers commented on how much they had learnt about the importance of product quality through their experiences in the laboratory. Conversely, control room workers spoke about mine site colleagues not understanding the complications that arose from the amount of water in the ore delivered to the plant. They claimed that if the mine site workers understood the problem, they could help overcome it by quite simple means. Equally, because they may lack an understanding of courtroom requirements, novice police officers may not make either appropriate or comprehensive enough notes at a crime scene to effect a prosecution when submitting evidence in court.

Consequently, a key component of the workplace curriculum is to identify and provide opportunities by which workers can best come to understand the requirements for their work. Many performance goals are likely to be readily accessible and can be understood in workplaces. When this is not possible, explicit interventions may need to be adopted to make these goals accessible and understandable. However, a limitation is that such measures may only be able to address routine work practices. The requirements for understanding non-routine practices may be more difficult. While totally novel tasks will remain unknown until encountered, it might be useful to make accessible the scope of the kinds of activities that may be encountered. The approach outlined by Dore and Sako (1989), with new tasks being considered as opportunities to learn more about work practice, could be adapted to develop further the capacity to enrich workers' knowledge in ways that would help them respond to new tasks. Principles arising from the need to provide access to goals are as follows:

- providing learners with access to the goals and sub-goals of work tasks in order to assist understanding what is required for performance;
- intentionally making accessible and explicit key elements of performance requirements;
- structuring support to assist learners in understanding the goals for work tasks; and
- intentionally outlining the scope of activities likely to be undertaken in the workplace (e.g. both the routine/non-routine).

In terms of learning:

- goals provide bases for approximations of activities and problem-solving activities;
- conceptualisations of goals provide an end-point for episodes of thinking and acting;
- goals provide a basis against which to monitor one's progress and performance.

Direct guidance of experts and others

The direct guidance of experts and more experienced others is central to the quality of workplace learning. Close guidance provides contributions that go beyond learning through indirect or direct modelling, such as imitation. The investigations into workplace learning referred to above emphasise the contributions to learning through shared problem-solving between the learner and expert others. Therefore, as depicted in Figure 4.1, there is a need for these kinds of interactions between more experienced coworkers and learners in the organisation of these learning experiences, and for monitoring to guard against inappropriate outcomes. The role of this direct guidance is fourfold. First, it can secure learners' access to a sequence of activities that are commensurate with the readiness of learners and the requirements for learning work practice. Second, direct guidance can guard against the development of inappropriate knowledge (e.g. bad habits, dangerous work practices). Third, it can provide access to and the development of knowledge that is hidden and/or difficult to learn without support and guidance. Fourth, learners are likely to be assisted by close guidance with the development of techniques and procedures used in the vocational practice (e.g. tricks of the trade). These roles are discussed in more detail below.

Securing access to activities
There are three identifiable parts to the task of securing appropriate access to workplace activities. The first is understanding learners' readiness for moving through the pathway of workplace activities. This requires an awareness of what the learners know and their ability to progress with tasks of increasing complexity and accountability. The ability to undertake a particular task with ease and consistently produce an acceptable outcome indicates a readiness to progress to a more complex activity. For instance, hairdressing apprentices' ability to competently place perming rods in clients' hair while conducting a conversation with the client indicates they have compiled these procedures. This ability demonstrates a readiness to progress to other tasks. Conversely, the apprentice who struggles with the task and has to use conscious thought to concentrate while undertaking both tasks probably needs more practice and is not ready to move on to the next task. As opportunities arise, decisions about learners' readiness will inevitably arise. The nature of the task, the learner's experiences and the consequences for both the task and the learner need to be considered. Associated with this role is management of the sequence of learning experiences as the learners engage in increasingly complex activities. The experienced coworker may be best placed to guide the timing and direction of the learners' experiences and progress. Part of the guidance role is to be an advocate for the learner, securing opportunities and easing the pathway to those activities. So, as with supervisors in the Japanese corporations, the more experienced coworker would be considering workplace activities in terms of the opportunities they present for the learning of others.

Guarding against inappropriate knowledge
As mentioned previously, not all learning that occurs in the workplace is appropriate or desirable. There is a need to guard against

novices learning inappropriate knowledge as part of everyday work activities. Learning unintended and undesirable knowledge is an inevitable outcome of learning through participation in everyday work activity, and some of this learning will directly influence how individuals conduct their work. However, through a process of monitoring and close guidance, other workers can assist in overcoming shortcomings such as hazardous short-cuts or dangerous work practices, or those habits that are ineffective or need improvement. Nevertheless, while monitoring the skills being learnt, care must be taken to permit learners to be self-regulated in addressing inappropriate practice. The workplace learning guide might ask the learner to critique their own performance as a means of understanding what is effective and less effective in their practice. Rather than telling, the use of close guidance can elicit responses and provide further direction. Through a process of monitoring and guidance, learners can guard against the development of inappropriate knowledge.

Accessing knowledge that is hidden

In the workplace, knowledge exists which is important to learn but may not be learnt alone. A particular instance is conceptual knowledge, which can be difficult to access because it is remote or hidden. There can also be important but hidden links among knowledge. For instance, in a restaurant kitchen, a chef might explain to a novice about the processes occurring when making a roux—fat and flour mixed together to thicken the sauce—because this understanding cannot develop unaided. The chef might extend this understanding by explaining the effects of adding either warm or cool liquids to the roux. In the secondary processing plant, experienced workers might use diagrammatic means to explain to new workers the processes occurring in the plant that may not be observable. Where knowledge is not available or accessible, some other means are required to make it accessible and comprehensible to learners. Vygotsky (1978) proposes that it is often complex knowledge that is least accessible, thereby requiring the assistance of a more experienced partner to ease the way to access. Consider, for instance, the complications that need to be accounted for in a large project (e.g. constructing a house, developing a database) or understanding a system (e.g. human physiology or the diagnosis of a patient). These kinds of understandings will probably require the guidance of a more experienced colleague to assist in their development.

Joint learning interactions will also be necessary where there are no set procedures that can usefully be learnt. The names of items, or symbols that have a particular meaning, fall into this category. Take, for instance, computer specifications. Unless you have an understanding of computer components, the details commonly provided in newspaper advertisements may be unfathomable. However, once an understanding develops of the terms being used and what the numerical ratings mean, you become a far more informed consumer. Also, where there are sets of linked concepts, some form of learner-focused activity may be useful, such as the deployment of intentional instructional strategies aimed to secure those associations. In Chapter 5, reference is made to strategies to assist the development of understanding in the workplace. These include questioning, the use of diagrams, analogies and explanations.

Close guidance in the development of procedures
Close guidance can also assist the development of procedures. Many vocational procedures are difficult to learn or refine unless they can be demonstrated, modelled and, possibly, remodelled. These procedures are often referred to as 'tricks of the trade' or heuristics, and they usually offer a means of securing a solution to a given task. Such techniques ease the process and reduce the demands of performing that task; however, they often require close guidance if they are to be learnt effectively. For instance, the chef who wishes to learn about Asian cooking can buy books full of recipes. However, these books are not always able to communicate the techniques required to cook this food authentically. Instead, working with someone skilled in cooking this food probably provides the best opportunity to observe and learn about the relevant techniques.

Although manuals often accompany pieces of equipment, they typically provide an account of what should happen and how you need to operate the equipment. Yet machines rarely malfunction as the manuals illustrate or predict. Nor can the range of potential malfunctions easily be captured and organised in text formats. One company had difficulties preparing its photocopy technicians (Orr 1987b, cited in Raizen 1994). The technicians were first equipped with detailed technical manuals for each type of machine. However, these manuals became so large that the information had to be converted to microfiche. Even this was not successful, because the required information was neither available nor accessible. Eventually, the company adopted a process based around access to experts' accounts of how the machines would probably malfunction and the procedures the experts adopted in fault-finding for and repairing these machines. The novice technicians first developed an understanding of the operation of the photocopier machines. Then, they were introduced to more experienced technicians who told them 'war stories' about the components most likely to malfunction and what to check first in order to save time and effort. These experienced technicians provided the novices with heuristics—procedures for diagnosing and repairing the photocopiers. They also probably developed diagnostic and problem-solving strategies based on ideas associated with the practice of repair, rather than manufacture. In the US Air Force, Gott (1995) identified heuristic use by expert avionics technicians when fault-finding with aircraft components. Instead of using manual-based approaches, they had developed their own 'least-effort' procedures from experience. For instance, these technicians initially tested the components that were easiest to access, before testing components that required more of the aircraft or its components to be dismantled. Such practice-derived procedures, while potent, are unlikely to be learnt other than through interactions with more expert technicians. In Chapter 5, workplace learning strategies for the development of procedures are specifically described, discussed and evaluated.

However, it is also necessary to consider in whom the quality of expertise, or being an 'expert other', is vested. The standing and credibility of the person nominated to provide direct guidance is likely to be important for the novices. Not surprisingly, evidence suggests that workers decide which coworkers possess the kinds of expertise they wish to develop and who they see as credible guides (Billett 1993a; Billett et al. 1998). Consequently, there can be no guarantee that workplace learners will grant this status to those nominated as workplace mentors or those labelled as 'trainers'. Enterprises often nominate supervisors as mentors or workplace guides, yet this is not always acceptable to the learners. Sometimes there are also concerns about these individuals' competence (i.e. they don't actually do the work, nor could they). In other situations, there are suspicions that learners are being appraised on performance for reasons other than those related to their learning (Billett et al. 1998). As proposed in Chapter 6, self-selection of guides for learning is likely to be the most effective approach in workplace situations. However, this is not always an accepted practice in enterprises. Other qualities of the expert's role as a learning guide also deserve consideration. First, the guide needs expertise in particular areas of work. At least three of the four tasks set out for experts in guiding the learning of others require rich knowledge of the work activity. More experienced coworkers have to provide access to specific knowledge and be able to model and coach procedures required in the workplace. Second, the experts have to be willing participants; and third, they have to be able to guide learning rather than be directive, as in teaching didactically (e.g. telling). Principles arising for guided learning are outlined below.

The roles of the expert other in the workplace are:

- securing access to experiences—determining readiness, sequencing of experiences and providing support for access;
- guarding against the learning of knowledge that is inappropriate—monitoring learners' experiences and outcomes;
- providing access to knowledge that is difficult to learn about—assisting access to knowledge that is hidden or opaque, or requires assistance to learn; and
- developing procedures through close interactions.

Principles associated with expert others as guides are:

- self-selection of guides or nominations by others are the most acceptable forms;
- qualities of experts as guides to learning:

(a) expertise in the area
(b) accessibility to learners
(c) willingness to guide, and
(d) can be persuaded to guide not always instruct.

Indirect guidance provided by the physical and social environment

As learners engage in everyday work activities, they continually access the indirect guidance provided by the workplace itself (see Figure 4.1). These activities are set in a social and physical environment that provides clues, cues and models to assist workplace learners. Observing experienced coworkers and peers serves as a model for performance. Even meal breaks provide an opportunity for workers to discuss and learn, and for novices to listen and learn about the work practice (Billett 1994b). The workplace itself voluntarily supports this development through the constant provision of clues and cues. These are provided in the form of access to opportunities to observe and listen to others and having visual access to artefacts in the workplace (e.g. completed and semi-completed products, their component parts, equipment, tools, procedures, etc.).

This indirect form of guidance (Lave 1990) also provides models of practice and standards by which learners can measure their progress. So, as learners engage in both routine and non-routine problem-solving activities in the workplace, they are guided indirectly by the contributions of the workplace environment. In particular, the ability to listen to and observe other workers is reported as being a most useful way to understand the requirements for practice (see Chapter 3). Equally, the structuring of work activities by the work practice and the cues for activity and clues for performance provided by the physical environment can provide another form of indirect guidance. However, as with direct guidance, some of the benefits of indirect guidance may not be available equally. If workers are physically or geographically isolated, opportunities to access and utilise indirect guidance may be quite limited. Hence it may be necessary for such workers to be encouraged or assisted to participate more fully.

Principles associated with indirect guidance are as follows. Learners require:

- opportunities to participate in work practice and activities;
- opportunities to interact with other workers and artefacts;
- routine access to goals and sub-goals; and
- engagement in discussion and practice in the workplace.

These four areas comprise the key elements of the workplace curriculum. Table 4.1 shows how the strengths and weaknesses of learning in workplaces as identified in Chapter 3 have been addressed in this model of workplace curriculum. The strengths have readily been incorporated into this model. Some weaknesses have also been addressed, as noted in Table 4.1. However, there are outstanding concerns that need to be addressed. They include:

- the unavailability of expertise;
- the reluctance of experts and others to assist learners; and
- the reluctance of individuals to participate.

These are personal and organisational factors. In Chapter 6, which focuses on managing and organising workplace learning, these concerns are examined in terms of encouraging participation and overcoming obstacles to participation. However, they remain key concerns for workplace learning arrangements. On the one hand, they influence the quality of guidance and access to activities. On the other, the degree to which individuals will participate effortfully in thinking and acting at work is related to the kinds of learning they will achieve.

Finally, there is also a need to consider that, at certain times and in particular circumstances, not all learning will take place most effectively through everyday activity in the workplace. Some knowledge is best acquired through other means. There are also situations where a model such as that outlined here will not be wholly applicable. For example, learning specific procedures such as keyboard skills or shorthand may best take place at college, with a teacher who knows the specific means of learning and perfecting such skills. This is not

Table 4.1 Contributions to a workplace curriculum

Contributions of workplace learning as identified in Chapter 3	How addressed within the model of workplace curriculum
Engagement in work tasks	Proposes a pathway of activities from which to move towards becoming a full participant or expert
Close guidance of other workers and experts	Provision of goals and procedures through direct guidance
The indirect guidance provided by the setting and practice within that setting	Provision for experiences in the workplace that provide access to models, clues and cues that aid performance with workplace tasks
Limitations of workplace learning	
Accessing inappropriate knowledge	Guidance and monitoring by more experienced coworkers to guard against learning inappropriate knowledge (see Chapter 5).
Access to activities	Structuring a pathway of activities from activities of low account-ability to those that are undertaken by full participants
Experts' reluctance to provide guidance	Needs to be addressed through the enterprise's organisation and management of workplace learning (see Chapter 6)
Unavailability of expert guidance	Needs to be addressed through the enterprise's organisation and management of workplace learning and provision of workplace expertise (see Chapters 5 and 6)
The development of understanding in the workplace	Direct guidance by more experienced coworkers including the use of selected strategies (questioning, diagrams, analogies) to enact conceptual change (Chapter 5)
The reluctance of individuals to engage	A pathway that is part of everyday activity, but needs to be more fully addressed in the organisation and management of workplace learn-ing at the enterprise level (Chapter 5)

to say that these skills cannot be learnt in the workplace. However, other forms of guidance can at least supplement this kind of learning. Another example might be developing conceptual knowledge that is both opaque and richly interlinked—for instance, nurses' learning of physiology, which may best take place in part in some environment other than a hospital ward. In other circumstances, such as noisy workplaces where close interactions are difficult, other kinds of interactions might have to be managed. Also, some workers are either physically or geographically separated (e.g. sales personnel, park wardens) from other workers and expert others. In these kinds of circumstances, where the integration of workplace-based and educationally based learning arrangements is possible, this provision may be the best option for learning. The preparation of nurses, trade-workers and professionals has long adopted this structured approach to initial vocational preparation, which has the potential to bring together the contributions of both kinds of environment.

DEVELOPING THE WORKPLACE CURRICULUM

Some elements of the workplace curriculum require little action. They are part of everyday work activities. However, the existence of work activities, other workers and the physical workplace provides the foundations for a more structured approach to learning in the workplace. To aid the task of structuring workplace activities and guidance, the requirements for the workplace curriculum have been set out in Table 4.2. These requirements are presented as principles for each element of the workplace curriculum. Responses for developing and enacting the workplace curriculum are identified in the middle column. Activities associated with the direct guidance and support provided by experienced coworkers and the roles required to organise and manage the workplace curriculum are presented in the right-hand column. These activities and roles are the principal focus of Chapter 5 and Chapter 6, respectively. However, it is the concerns associated with a set of workplace experiences (the contents of the middle column) that are the focus of this section. These concerns are:

- identifying a pathway of activities premised on their complexity and accountability;
- identifying important goals and sub-goals (factors) for performance;
- identifying the scope of activities (non-routine as well as routine activities);
- identifying knowledge that is difficult to learn;
- accessing everyday decision-making; and
- structuring access to these activities.

As part of developing a workplace curriculum, there needs to be an understanding of what comprises effective performance in the workplace. This includes the sequencing of work activities that need to be undertaken, the way they are to be performed and those things that are difficult to learn in these activities. To understand these factors requires an analysis of the work activities. However, it is important that such an analysis accounts for both an explication of existing practice ('what is') and an informed view of what is desirable ('what should be'). An analysis of existing practice provides useful information for organising the workplace curriculum. However, this information may be augmented by contributions about what is currently being practised, and it can thus be changed to improve workplace goals.

A range of strategies exists for gathering information about work. These include the use of surveys, interviews, observation, critical incident interviews, task analysis, etc. The degree to which the analysis of work in the enterprise needs to be highly detailed and documented is likely to be determined by the scope of the enterprise's activities and its need to detail these requirements. The assumption adopted here is that some identification and detailing of pathways, goals for learning and components of work that are difficult to learn would be useful in most workplace learning situations. However, more elaborate processes can be undertaken. For instance, some enterprises may wish to link their safety and/or quality systems and arrangements for career advancement to the learning curriculum. Collaborative arrangements are those most likely to engage workers fully and productively and to lead to mutual understandings.

The detailing of pathways indicates the requirements for performance in the workplace. Identification of work tasks that are difficult to learn represents the minimum approach required to structure effective learning activities in the workplace. Overall, the scope of the development task is to:

- delineate work areas;
- determine the requirements for performance;
- develop a pathway or pathways of activities; and
- identify tasks of work that are difficult to learn about.

These tasks are discussed in the following sections.

Identifying the work area

An initial identification of the work area(s) which will be the focus of the workplace curriculum needs to be undertaken. This establishes a basis for determining who should be providing information about work, what information should be gathered, the scope of the work tasks being performed and the requirements for expert performance. None of this can proceed unless there is some understanding of the work area(s) under review. As proposed in Chapter 2, each workplace has different—probably unique—requirements for performance. Beyond understanding what has to be learnt through work, these requirements can also inform the selection of particular learning strategies. In some workplaces, the use of technology or the vocational practice being deployed can make some learning tasks difficult. Hence strategies to make this knowledge more accessible may be needed. There may also be different focuses for learning. In some workplaces, it may be about the continuity of established procedures, whereas in others it might be about the management of new procedures and work practices. Some enterprises have stable workforces, whereas in others there is a constant need to orient and induct new employees.

There are also variations in delineating work area(s). Identifying a work area might best be premised on work functions. For instance, in the secondary processing plant referred to earlier, there were

Table 4.2 Curriculum development activities, guidance of learners and organisation of experiences in the workplace

Sets of needs	Developmental activity (Chapter 4)	Other support (Chapters 5 and 6)
Movement from peripheral to full participation		
Movement from less to more complex tasks	Identifying a pathway of activities (complexity and accountability) Providing guided access to activities	Providing guided access to activities
Movement from less to more accountable tasks	Identifying key goals and sub-goals for performance Providing guided access to activities	Providing guided access to activities
Provision of experiences to understanding the goals and procedures required for performance	Identifying key goals and sub-goals for performance Providing guided access to activities	
Access to goals for performance		
Access to goals required for performance	Identifying key goals and sub-goals for performance	Providing access to sub-goals and goals
Access the factors required for performance	Identifying key factors for performance	
Structure support to understand goals for activities		Providing guided access to activities
Understand the scope of workplace activities (routine–non-routine)	Identifying non-routine as well as routine activities Providing guided access to activities	Accessing the scope of activities

Direct guidance of experts and others		
Securing access to experiences (determining readiness, sequencing of experiences and providing support for access)	Providing guided access to activities	Understanding readiness and providing guided access and monitoring of learner
Monitoring learner to guard against inappropriate learning		Guidance in the access and monitoring of development
Providing access to difficult-to-learn knowledge (hidden or opaque)	Identifying knowledge that is difficult to learn	Providing access to knowledge that is difficult to learn about
Developing procedures through close interactions		Guidance in the development of procedures
Indirect guidance provided by the workplace		
Opportunities to participate and interact in work practice and activities	Identifying a pathway of activities (complexity and accountability)	Guided opportunities to participate and interact
	Providing guided access to activities	
Routine access to goals and sub-goals	Structuring opportunities to interact with others	
Engaging in the discussion and practice in the workplace	Access to everyday decision-making	

clearly delineated work areas, such as the control room, calcification area, furnace room and mine site. As well as being physically separate, each of these work areas had distinct and discernible sets of skill requirements. In other workplaces, such as coal mines, some work is organised in terms of workplace production functions for some workers (e.g. process workers in removal of overburden, drilling, blasting, coal washing). However, other work has functions applicable across all work areas (e.g. tradeworkers in fitting/turning, diesel fitting and vehicle maintenance). Some workplaces have highly heterogenous work tasks—for example, railway systems and local government, with their quite distinct areas of work. Other work situations may be quite homogenous, with lots of workers doing the same or similar tasks. Many production facilities are of this kind, with groups of workers conducting the same practice. Hairdressing salons, for instance, usually comprise an entire practice in themselves. The work may be quite homogenous, and therefore does not need to be delineated. Some smaller businesses or workplaces may also be of this kind. Yet delineating areas and pathways for development does not negate the prospect of offering multiple and different kinds of pathways for learners. For example, nurses in their hospital-based preparation have experiences in hospital wards with quite distinct functions or focuses. However, they are able to experience a range of contexts in which nursing is conducted, and later are able to specialise in particular areas. To reiterate, the purposes of delineating work practice for development are:

- to understand the ways in which work is homogenous or discrete and distinct;
- to understand its requirements, which then become the focus for learning in enterprises; and
- to develop an appreciation of the kinds of knowledge that need to be learnt.

Sources of information

Diverse sources of information about the requirements for work are available to develop the workplace curriculum. These may include written documents—such as quality assurance standards, industry competency standards, job descriptions and duty statements—plus the outcomes of any work analyses that have been conducted. Often, however, these are statements of intent, reflecting ideals rather than reality. Therefore, they need to be used in conjunction with other sources of information about the scope and requirements of work tasks. Clearly, it is desirable to gather information from those who actually undertake the work activities and those who have journeyed towards full participation (e.g. experts, supervisors). These individuals are best placed to provide information about current performance ('what is') and also to be canvassed on how work should ideally be undertaken ('what should be'). Gaining insights from interviews and observations of those actually performing the work tasks is likely to be the most instructive way to proceed. However, be cautious in gathering this information. The means of gathering data should be sensitive to the individuals' participation in the activities and culture within the workplace. Many of those informants may be unused to this task and see themselves to be 'on trial'. Gathering of the data may thus need to be undertaken supportively, with cues being provided to assist in eliciting the required information. Sheets with questions to be considered can be distributed prior to any interviews, and cues about the desirable scope of responses to questions might be useful to guide the responses.

Language and terminology also need to be appropriate for participants and must be mindful of workplace sensitivities. For instance, the term 'expert' is used pejoratively in some workplaces. Consequently, participants described as experts may be made uncomfortable by such a designation or, when asked what it means to be an expert, may respond accordingly. The use of the term 'experienced worker' may be a safer option. The use of grounded approaches, such as getting participants to think of actual instances, is likely to assist the quality of the information elicited. For example, participants might be requested to identify an individual whom they believe is highly skilled. Then they could be asked to describe the qualities that make this person a competent performer. Those who are experienced (e.g. experts) may be the best source of information when defining what it means to be skilled in the workplace, as well as in regard to the tasks that are difficult to learn about and the pathways of activities required for full participation.

In Appendix 1, some examples of questions used to elicit this information are provided. This information will typically refer to the actual practice—or 'what is'—which is exactly the purpose of gathering this information. However, questions can be used to elicit views on what 'should be' as well as what currently occurs. These items might be as simple as asking 'what should be happening' after asking about what currently occurs. In addition, asking relative newcomers about the pathway of activities they have participated in (the learning curriculum) and what activities they found most difficult to learn would draw usefully on recent experiences. Collectively, these sources can be used to describe the scope of the workplace tasks, and identify a pathway to full participation. Because not everything that happens in workplaces is wholly desirable or appropriate, some justification of views about how work should proceed is probably required. For instance, a small group of workers could be interviewed in detail and then their aggregated contributions distributed to a wider group for comment (e.g. errors, additions and deletions).

Adopting a collaborative approach to data-gathering is likely to be instrumental (Sefton 1993), although overcoming distrust and scepticism may be an outcome of the process rather than a starting point. Darrah (1996), for instance, notes how interactions between technicians and production staff resulted in reciprocal learning about each other's work. Technicians were informed about the complex requirements for production workers to reach output goals. Equally, and conversely, the production staff learnt to use diagnostic software far more effectively through understanding its purpose and operations. These actions resulted in making production testing more efficient and effective. This outcome was premised on mutuality of concerns and reciprocity of learning. However, if these are not evident, opportunities for collaboration may be restricted. In the secondary processing plant (Billett 1994b), interventions by engineers were seen as disempowering by the production workers because they were directed in what they had to do rather than being consulted. This approach ignored the fact that the very individuals who were supposed to implement the engineers' directions believed they knew more about the plant's operation than the engineers. Consequently, these production workers remained sceptical of what they were told to do and frustrated that their expertise was routinely ignored and overridden.

Scope of activities

Being able to identify the scope of the routine and non-routine tasks of the workplace provides a basis for organising the pathway towards full participation. This requires gaining an understanding of the scope of workplace activities. Asking workers what tasks they perform daily, weekly, monthly, yearly and over a period of years can be used to identify the scope of their activities. However, some prompting may be required. Experience indicates that workers will often provide quite limited responses. However, lists of tasks can be used as prompts to assist these workers, either in conjunction with the initial questions or after they have attempted an initial recall of the scope of the work tasks. In a similar way, they can also be asked about tasks they are required to know about, although they may never have to use the information—for instance, being prepared to engage in emergency situations. Again, it may be necessary to provide some support for participants to identify the scope and frequency of the work tasks.

It is also desirable to identify what it means to be an expert or full participant in the work practice, as this can provide the goals for learning. The degree of detail is likely to be situation dependent, and therefore needs to be undertaken in each workplace. As mentioned already, broad characteristics of expert performance are likely to be forthcoming from the participants who are familiar with the workplace and able to identify the qualities of expert workers in that workplace.

Delineating the learning pathway

Delineating the learning pathway includes identifying the sequences of activities in which individuals engaged during their passage towards full participation (see Figure 4.1). This draws upon the understanding of what it means to be an expert, the tasks (and knowledge) required to be learnt along the way to becoming an expert, and the need to identify those activities or understandings that are difficult to learn. The actual process of identifying the pathway of experiences may be as simple as determining the sequence in which experts believed they acquired their skills and comparing this with the experiences of recent learners. This information can be used and refined to generate an effective pathway of learning, together with structuring opportunities to access both the process (means of securing goals) and the product (what those goals are).

In the hairdressing study, both the scope and the pathway of activities were determined by giving each of the hairdressers a survey-type document that had a list of hairdressing activities and competencies. These statements were taken from a curriculum document for the hairdressing industry (see Appendix 2 for an example). The hairdressers were asked to respond to this document by indicating whether the particular task was undertaken by an expert hairdresser or a fourth-year, third-year or second-year apprentice. Variations on this approach could include sets of statements about the scope of work tasks elicited in the workplace, with experts or experienced workers being asked to sequence them as they had learnt them and also indicate which tasks were difficult to learn (see Appendix 3). In all instances, it will be necessary to gather information from a number of workers in order to validate the pathway. There will inevitably be some differences across responses, but patterns should emerge that indicate a pathway of activities in the form of clusters of activities (see Figure 4.1).

Proposed statements about scope of activities and pathways can be distributed for comment and refinement. As stated earlier, it may not be necessary for there to be a lockstep access to each set of activities. Rather, there is a need to structure a progression of experiences which can be accessed and which are progressively within the learners' Zone of Proximal Development (Vygotsky 1978)—what they are able to achieve with the assistance of a more expert worker. Therefore, work activities can be grouped that are deemed appropriate to be undertaken at any particular point in time, and as they become available in the workplace. Further, the development of this pathway of experiences should identify goals for performance and the tasks that are particularly difficult to learn.

Goals for performance and where learning is hard

Tasks requiring knowledge that is difficult to learn need to be identified, so they can attract direct guidance from more experienced workers. The listing of the scope and sequencing of the pathway of activities provides a basis for these to be identified. This identification is central to guiding the focus for interventions to make these goals explicit. Firstly, they have to be understood; and secondly, action needs to be taken to make them explicit in the workplace curriculum. For a grounded approach to structuring the responses of the workers to questions specifically designed to elicit this information, see Appendixes 1 and 2. Appendix 2 comprises a list of tasks where workers were encouraged to indicate the sequence in which tasks should be learnt (the workplace curriculum) and which of these tasks were particularly difficult to learn. Workers usually have little difficulty identifying the key goals for performance, and which tasks are likely to be difficult (see Appendix 3). Understanding what is difficult to learn and the requirements for performance aid the design of the learning curriculum through identifying areas required for particular interventions to assist the learning. The gathering of information, as described above, does not need to be onerous—much of it can be undertaken through a two-phase process involving gathering information from recent learners and experts, collating that information and then sharing it with other workers for verification and modification.

In sum, such an analysis will generate rich information about vocational tasks, their relationship to a particular work practice and also how a workplace curriculum might proceed. In doing so, it advocates curriculum intent, formulates a sequence of experiences to achieve that intent and provides a means to determine whether such goals are being achieved.

LEGITIMATING THE WORKPLACE CURRICULUM

The model of a workplace curriculum presented above has been developed from the findings of investigations into learning in workplaces and is informed by theories of learning and instruction. Indeed, there is a long tradition of basing the learning of vocations in work activities—one example is apprenticeships. Dewey (1916) advocated that the only way to learn about occupations was through occupations and making the most of immediate experiences and opportunities in this learning. He specifically referred to realising individuals' full potential through vocational endeavours, while cautioning against learning with short-term outcomes. As noted earlier, Lave (1990) has illustrated how work practice itself constitutes a pathway of activities (and hence learning experiences) that she referred to as the 'learning curriculum'. This is a view of curriculum premised on the learners' activities rather than based on direct teaching.

However, despite all this, there may be some reluctance to accept the legitimacy of a workplace curriculum, largely because the term 'curriculum' is usually associated with educational institutions. For instance, definitions of curriculum often make explicit reference to formalised programs of study in educational institutions or achieving the institutional goals. Typically, these conceptions also refer to curriculum being associated with determining the intents for learning (aims, goals and objectives); what is to be learnt (content); how that learning will proceed (method); and judgments about the outcomes of the learning (evaluation). However, there are also definitions of curriculum that de-emphasise the educational institution, instead focusing on the learners. Some of these definitions see curriculum as something experienced by the learner through the activities in which they engage. Posner (1982) proposes that the tasks in which students engage structure what information they select from a situation and how they process that information. Thereby he advocates a view of curriculum premised on participation in activities to guide learning effectively. This approach is supported by what Rogoff and Lave (1984) concluded from investigations of learning through everyday activities: that activity structures cognition. That is, the activities in which we engage influence how we think, act and therefore learn. Collins et al. (1989: 487) advance four reasons why activities can legitimately be seen as a basis for organising learning. They claim that:

- learners come to understand the purposes and use of the knowledge they are learning;
- they learn by actively using the knowledge rather than passively receiving it;
- they learn the different conditions under which their knowledge can be applied; and
- learning in multiple contexts induces the abstraction of knowledge so that its use can extend beyond the circumstances in which it is constructed.

These views are consonant with the constructivist perspective adopted here, with its focus on the activities and interactions that learners experience.

Even conceptions of curriculum as they relate to educational institutions are not wholly inconsistent with the conception of a workplace curriculum advanced here. It too is concerned with intents (i.e. developing expertise), the content of the learning (i.e. what is required to be learnt for expertise in a workplace and vocation), method (i.e. guided participation in increasingly accountable activities) and evaluation (i.e. whether the learning will be robust enough for individuals and enterprises). Learning in the workplace has intentional elements. Just as in educational institutions, it is structured or 'formalised' in ways that organise and distribute opportunities to learn.

There are also strong associations among teaching, teachers and curriculum. Teachers have been described as 'curriculum makers' (Schwab 1970) because they determine and respond to learners' needs in enacting the curriculum. However, there is some divergence between this conception and the model of the workplace curriculum proposed above, because the focus is on activities and guidance by more expert workers. Teachers, as such, are absent from what is proposed. Nevertheless, in the workplace curriculum, experienced coworkers are proposed as guiding and monitoring other workers' learning experiences. This guidance extends to the use of instructional strategies—a role undertaken by teachers in schools, colleges and universities. In these ways, a curriculum premised on workplace activities and guidance by more experienced coworkers is not as far removed from popular conceptions of curriculum as it might at first appear to be. Certainly, the overall concerns of curriculum—intentional learning, the organisation of learning experiences, methods of learning and means of evaluating learning—are all addressed in the model of workplace curriculum. Indeed, the idea of learners in the workplace progressing along pathways of learning experiences is consistent with the Latin origins of the word 'curriculum' which refers to 'a course to run'— a *currere*.

However, there are distinctions between the school pedagogy and that of the workplace. One difference is the organisation of learning opportunities. In the workplace, the key emphasis is on learning through work activities as they arise, rather than through the activities deliberately organised and implemented by teachers in educational institutions. This goes some way towards explaining why teachers whose expertise resides in classroom-based activities are not an integral component of this model of curriculum. Instead, the approach adopted here is akin to apprenticeships—which, according to Collins et al. (1989: 491), 'is the way we learn most naturally. It characterises learning before there were schools, from learning one's language to learning to run an empire.' Activities and the guidance of others, as well as the social and physical environment, are the key components of this model of curriculum. Together, these present key curriculum and instructional design principles.

Nevertheless, in proposing a workplace curriculum as a legitimate conception, it is necessary to consider Dewey's (1916) concern about short-term outcomes from such learning. What is learnt in the workplace is likely to be perceived by many to be reductive and instrumental. These concerns are real, raising the issue of which orientations can best be used to describe a curriculum for the workplace. It is through such a consideration that values associated with a workplace curriculum can be discussed.

ORIENTATIONS OF THE WORKPLACE CURRICULUM

The stated goal for the workplace curriculum is the development of individuals' vocational expertise. Correspondingly, its focus is on the development of robust vocational knowledge applicable to work situations of a specific vocation. As such, it might be viewed as being technicist—merely reproductive—or cognitivist because of its goal of developing problem-solving capacities in individuals. Others will likely refer to the need for a workplace curriculum to be intentionally emancipatory—that is, seeking to develop critical insights about work practice. The difficulty with labelling its orientation as technicist, cognitive, interpretivist or socially critical is that, in different ways, it embraces all of these orientations.

Workplace learning as technicist

The model of curriculum proposed here aims to respond to the requirement of a particular work practice. It seeks to assist learners to 'reproduce' practices that are skilful and constitute effective ways of working in that practice. Consequently, it is reproductive in this sense and can also be categorised as being instrumental, facilitating the learning of the knowledge through practice. However, such learning may also be personally and socially emancipatory through its capacity to develop skilfulness and provide opportunities for insights that are not wholly reproductive. Although learning through modelled behaviour and imitation is a key component of the workplace curriculum, individuals still interpret and select what and how they learn. It is possible to suggest that learning is unlikely ever to be reproductive given the active but interpretative base of individuals' learning. Also, learning from others who are competent highlights the positive aspects of reproductive types of learning. Learning instrumentally to become a full participant may be essential and even emancipatory for groups who are under-represented as full participants in a particular occupation, such as work.

Lynch (1993), however, has also identified factors that mark key differences in the relationship between individuals participating in educational institutions and workers learning in the workplace.

She proposes that the two workplace agents—the enterprise and the individual—have different goals, access to resources and preferences. Consequently, the nature of what is going to be offered may be less negotiable than in educational environments. What experiences the enterprise is willing to make available are associated with its strategic or even short-term goals. For instance, workplace-based vocational education programs may fail to allow students (employees) to fulfil the course requirements, therefore inhibiting them from obtaining certification (Billett & Hayes 1999). If employers select only those modules that reflect enterprises' needs, the requirements for certification may remain unfulfilled. The employees/students are often unable to complete the remaining modules required for certification because they are only offered through the workplace. Whether the enterprises are just being parsimonious with module selection or are concerned to restrict their employees' mobility is not always clear. An unfortunate feature of this arrangement is that these workers are from an industry sector that has traditionally been denied both vocational education provisions and formal certification. Hence these workers have been, and remain, structurally disadvantaged. The establishment of work-based courses has opened the door to these workers who have not had the opportunity to seek formal certification, only to see the actions of an employer frustrate this goal. So, although the technicist orientation of workplace learning can provide opportunities for personal development for workers denied other means, it can also be enacted in ways that limit and frustrate these outcomes.

Workplace learning as cognitivist

Given that the aim of the workplace curriculum is to develop adaptable and robust (transferable) learning, not restricted to routine vocational performances in a particular workplace, it can be seen as cognitive in orientation. The evidence suggests that there are clear and robust cognitive consequences for participation in everyday activities (e.g. Rogoff & Lave 1984; Gauvain 1993; Billett 1995; Billett et al. 1998). The knowledge learnt through these means is not wholly restricted to the circumstances in which it was constructed. Through the development of transferable knowledge, the ability to respond to new situations, to consistently produce goods and services of prescribed quality and to adapt to changing circumstances should be achievable. These cognitive attributes are central to individuals' vocational development and progress, as well as to enterprises' current and future performance in responding to the changing requirements for effective work practices.

Workplace learning as interpretivist

To resist further learning at work necessarily being viewed as wholly reproductive, it needs to be re-emphasised that learning through work is neither socialisation nor enculturation. Learners unquestioningly learn what they experience. This is because learners are interpretative and selective about the knowledge they learn and how that knowledge is learnt. Ideas such as the co-construction of knowledge (Valisner 1994) and co-participation in practice (Billett 1999a) refer to the mutual transformation of both the object and the subject in the learning process. Even under coercion, individuals may come to master knowledge that they do not necessarily believe (Wertsch 1998). However, they will not appropriate this knowledge—'make it their own' (Leontiev 1981)—instead feigning compliance in public demonstrations and utterances while remaining unconvinced and uncommitted in practice (Wertsch 1998). Similarly, it is incorrect to assume that the formation of a vocational identity through participation will result unquestioningly from participation at work, as Lave and Wenger (1991) propose. Instead, participation can lead to disidentification with the social practice in which individuals engage (e.g. Hodges 1998), particularly when the values of work practice are inconsonant with those of the individual. Again, this is exemplified in the reluctance of workers from a Vietnamese heritage to engage in teamwork in a manufacturing plant (Darrah 1997). Therefore, learning through work can be seen as being in part interpretivist.

Workplace learning as socially critical

An approach to curriculum is not socially critical or emancipatory simply because it is labelled as such, or because it claims this as its goal. Instead, the quality of the learning, interactions and outcomes determines whether these intentions are realised. Certainly, there is little evidence to suggest that an outcome of learning in workplaces is that workers appropriate workplace-based knowledge unquestioningly. Nor are workplace experiences immune to questioning of the purposes of and goals for such learning experiences. Interactions in workplaces are set within inherently contested terrain, as proposed earlier. Those contestations are between owners/management and workers (e.g. Danford 1998), different affiliations of workers (Billett 1995b), workplace cliques, old-timers and newcomers (Lave & Wenger 1991), males and females (Tam 1997; Probert 1999) and part-time and full-time workers (Berhardt 1999). As such, interactions at work sit within critical relations that are ubiquitous and the influences of which can be profound. For instance, some enterprises' managements are nervous about a highly empowered workforce. Hence, when management curtails apparently more effective practice which also reduces management control, an important lesson is learnt. Workers' scepticism about workplace relations and the intents of employers is not easily dissipated (Danford 1998). Nor are workers passive and obliging respondents to employers' goals (Butler 1999). In some instances, quite the opposite occurs—for example, workers in a manufacturing plant expressing concern about the enterprise-specificity of their employer-sponsored training (Billett & Hayes 1998). As already noted, coal miners viewed management's safety training programs as a means of transferring the responsibility for mine site safety to them (Billett 1995b). Furthermore, workplaces afford asymmetrical opportunities for access to activities, guidance, support and recognition. Issues of gender (Tam 1997; Probert 1999), race (Hull 1997), personal affiliation, differentials in the valuing of particular work activities (Darrah 1997) and other factors determine how individuals are able to participate in workplace practices and therefore learn at work.

Importantly, the learning of vocational practice can be personally empowering, as it can broaden individuals' options and potential directions. For many categories of workers, workplaces offer the best prospect of learning work-related knowledge and developing that practice further. Indeed, for many workers, there is simply no other option than to learn in workplaces. Consequently, the provisions of structured learning in the workplace—particularly when it is formally recognised—offer a prospect of preparation and recognition that, for many workers, is unavailable elsewhere. The contested nature of workplaces, how individuals learn and the opportunities afforded by workplaces to learn together suggest that there are many dimensions of socially contested and yet generative outcomes from learning at work. Consequently, a curriculum model premised on participation in social practice has the potential to be emancipatory and engender socially critical outcomes.

SUMMARY

This chapter has described the elements of the workplace curriculum based around the dual principles of accessing activities and guidance. This concept can best be described as guided learning at work. The components of the model have deliberately been set out to maximise the contributions of everyday participation in the workplace. However, the structuring of these experiences is required in order to both improve the contributions of everyday participation at work and address some identified shortcomings of learning through work. Structuring a workplace curriculum leads to inevitable concerns about the best way to develop and implement it. Accordingly, a process has been developed comprising the identification of the pathways of activities, the requirements for performance (work goals) and those activities or knowledges that are difficult to learn. This kind of development can only occur in a situation where the work practice can be understood, as the requirements for work are a product of such situations. Moreover—and given the inevitable concerns about the legitimacy of a workplace curriculum—it is necessary for it to be positioned as conceptually and theoretically sound.

In the next two chapters, important factors contributing to implementing the workplace curriculum are outlined. In Chapter 5, the focus on guided learning proposes how more experienced coworkers can guide the learning of less experienced workers. In Chapter 6, issues associated with the effective management and organisation of a workplace curriculum as part of the learning process are discussed.

5

Guided learning at work

GUIDED LEARNING

The kinds of expert guidance provided to less experienced workers will have a direct influence on the quality of learning in the workplace. In particular, guidance in the form of direct interactions and collaborative problem-solving can help develop the robust knowledge required for vocational expertise. Such guidance includes helping individuals learn knowledge that they might not be able to access alone and providing insights into work and procedures for conducting that work effectively. These outcomes are important for enterprises and are worthy of sponsorship within them. The more easily workers are able to complete routine tasks and respond effectively to new tasks, the more productive the enterprise is likely to be. Consequently, it is worthwhile for enterprises to develop guided learning as part of everyday work practice, and to intentionally structure and prepare for such learning. Much of the effectiveness of the workplace curriculum lies in the quality of the guided learning provided. Such is the significance of this guidance role that the approach to learning outlined in this book has been referred to as guided learning at work. Accordingly, there is a need to examine the role of guided learning, how it is enacted and how its usefulness can be appraised.

Guidance at work can take a number of forms, ranging from being a mentor who guides and supports an individual's career trajectory over a period of years, to assisting a novice in unfamiliar tasks, through to being a role model in the avoidance of detrimental behaviour (Garvey 1994; Gay 1994). The form of guidance focused on here involves more experienced or expert workers assisting in the development of the vocational practice of less experienced workers. These learners could be novices, those working their way towards expert performance or workers from another work area broadening their skills. Three levels of guidance have been identified as constituting this role: (a) organising and managing learners' experiences in the workplace; (b) close guidance in the development of procedures and understanding associated with work practice; and (c) the development of self-regulated learning and the transfer of working knowledge to new tasks and other workplaces.

The first level of guidance comprises the selection of experiences, organising access to those experiences and monitoring learners' development of performance on a pathway of activities. These activities will take the learner towards expert performance via the pathways of the workplace curriculum, as proposed in the previous chapter. The guide's role at this level includes organising learning opportunities, guiding learners by selecting and monitoring their participation in workplace activities and determining their readiness to engage in activities of increasing accountability. This level largely consists of enacting activities identified as constituting the workplace curriculum, as proposed in Chapter 4.

The second level of guidance is concerned with developing the knowledge required for accomplishing workplace tasks and goals. It emphasises direct guidance as a means to assist learning through engagement in collaborative problem-solving in the workplace. The use of modelling, coaching, scaffolding and fading by learning guides is proposed to assist learners to gain proficiency in workplace tasks, through guided participation in these tasks. Fading refers to the gradual removal of support until learners can perform the learnt task independently (see below for further explanation of these techniques). Also included in this level of guidance are other guided learning strategies which aim to develop understanding about practice. These strategies are used to provide access to learning that would otherwise have remained hidden. They include questioning dialogues, diagrams and analogies, and again are intended for use in the context and practice of everyday work activities.

The third level of guidance seeks to make transferable to other situations and practice the knowledge learnt in a particular workplace. It focuses on developing individuals' ability to transfer knowledge and be self-regulating in predicting, monitoring and evaluating their work accomplishments, and therefore their learning. Strategies such as reflection and considering the scope of the applicability of what has been learnt can assist this process and render individuals' knowledge robust and transferable. These attributes are important if individuals are to be able to respond to new tasks in their workplaces as well as transfer their knowledge to other work ⅄ practices. So, following what has been proposed in Chapter 3 and building upon the organisation of learning experiences in Chapter 4, the requirements for guided learning in workplaces are as follows.

First level of guidance (see Chapter 4)
- organising and sequencing of workplace experiences (the learning curriculum—sequencing tasks which take the learner from being a novice to an expert, and from peripheral involvement to full participation in the workplace);
- providing access to ongoing autonomous practice (e.g. access to routine and non-routine activities);
- monitoring learners' readiness to progress on the pathways of activities of increasing accountability and complexity; and
- providing access to goals and sub-goals associated with the work practice (e.g. important goals and understanding of requirements for performance).

Second level of guidance
- modelling of tasks to be performed and access to goals to be learnt (e.g. access to experiences which make available the

opportunity to understand the required standard for the completed task);

- demonstrating procedures (e.g. physical demonstration of task procedures, including demonstrating and modelling the level of performance required);
- coaching with procedures associated with the activity (assisting with joint problem-solving to secure successful outcomes for the learner; providing appropriate levels of support depending on the requirements for task completion);
- making accessible knowledge that is hidden (using strategies to make accessible that conceptual knowledge that is remote from the learner and is unlikely to be learnt without intervention from expert others); and
- monitoring learners' progress and avoidance of learning inappropriate knowledge.

Third level of guidance
- engaging learners in opportunities to reflect on what they have learnt;
- encouraging the comparison of individuals' progress with that of others;
- assisting learners to understand the breadth of the applicability of what they have learnt; and
- facilitating the abstraction of learning from one situation to another.

Together, these levels comprise the kinds of workplace guidance that aim to develop transferable vocational knowledge. This guidance, wherever possible, is to be conducted as part of everyday activity at work. Through this, the tasks of working and learning are drawn together in circumstances where the requirements for work are accessible, and where the consequences for and contributions of work are observable and can be used to provide important feedback for learners. To different degrees, such guidance will already be occurring in workplaces. This is particularly likely to be the case where on-the-job learning is organised—as, for instance, between tradeworkers and their apprentices. However, to realise its full potential, the guided learning role will require expert workers to be intentionally and thoroughly prepared as learning guides. This preparation will particularly need to focus on using the strategies that comprise the second and third levels of guidance.

GUIDED LEARNING IN THE WORKPLACE

What are the reasons for considering a guided approach to learning, rather than one which emphasises direct teaching? Learning is an active process which is influenced by external contributions but ultimately determined and regulated by individuals. These realisations have led to the conclusion that the effectiveness of direct teaching may have been overestimated (Brown & Palinscar 1989; Rogoff 1990, 1995). Accordingly, the emerging goal for instruction is to find ways of placing the task of, and responsibility for, learning upon learners themselves. At the same time, they need to be supported in order to guide the kinds of learning that occur. This has led to the use of guided methods of instruction in schools. These methods include the reciprocal teaching of reading (Brown & Palinscar 1989), the procedural facilitation of writing (Bereiter & Scardamalia 1987), Schoenfield's (1985) method of teaching mathematical problemsolving and the cognitive apprenticeship for teaching reading, writing and mathematics (Collins et al. 1989). These approaches to instruction emphasise the expert facilitation of learning through processes of guiding learners to think and act as experts would. Interestingly, the genesis of these methods lies in the way learning proceeds in workplaces. Bereiter and Scardamalia (1989) and Collins et al. (1989) both modelled their methods directly on apprenticeship learning in workplaces. Both methods intend to develop learners' ability to think and act like experts by modelling how experts conduct tasks and assist learners (in different ways) to learn these expert approaches to thinking.

Significantly, many aspects of traditional approaches to learning for vocations have been adopted in these kind of models. For instance, more than two decades ago, Kalusmeier and Goodwin

(1975) proposed six instructional activities required for the development of a skill:

- to analyse the skill in terms of the learner's abilities and developmental level;
- to demonstrate the correct response;
- to guide initial responses verbally and physically;
- to arrange for appropriate practice;
- to provide informational feedback and correct inadequate responses; and
- to encourage independent evaluation.

The existence of an expert, engagement in activities, the guidance and encouragement of experts and the deliberate generation of self-monitoring skills are key ingredients of this instructional strategy. Perhaps the cognitive apprenticeship approach of Collins et al. (1989) has best elaborated this guided approach to learning. Their model of learning aims to develop the procedures and conceptual knowledge required for performance and the self-monitoring and self-correction skills required for expertise. These outcomes are highly consistent with the aims and procedures of the second and third levels of guided learning in the workplace. Components of the cognitive apprenticeship approach—modelling, coaching, scaffolding and fading—are used as a means of describing the second level of guided learning. As indicated in Figure 5.1, a sequential use of these strategies in work settings is proposed. They are discussed in this order.

Modelling

Modelling is the process whereby experts perform a task with learners observing and building a mental model of the demonstrated task and the requirements for performance. Modelling assists the learning of tasks through making the requirements for performance accessible. This includes the identification of the sub-tasks to be learnt and the goals for those sub-tasks, which collectively lead to the mature performance of the task. As Kalusmeier and Goodwin (1975) have stated, the accepted procedure for skill development is to first demonstrate

Source: Collins et al. (1989)

Figure 5.1 Cognitive apprenticeship model

the task at its normal level of performance (e.g. pace) in order to illustrate the overall goal and standard for performance. This demonstration is then followed by other demonstrations, performed at a slower pace. These allow learners to understand the separate phases (sub-tasks) of the task and how they are performed. In demonstrating a bricklaying task, for instance, the expert might model the processes of lifting the brick, placing the cement on each end and quickly aligning and laying the brick on the wall. This demonstration is then followed by one that is slower and models how bricks are best held and the amount of cement gathered onto the bricklayer's trowel. Next, they show how to position the brick for cement to be placed on it, the brick's alignment and placement on the wall and the use of the trowel to position the brick into its desired position. The principle here is one of modelling first for an understanding of the overall performance, then developing an understanding of the component parts of the task.

To take another example, in instructing someone how to change gears in a car, a demonstration might first allow the novice driver to understand the requirement for smoothness, ease and speed of the gear change. This could be followed by a demonstration permitting the novice to understand different stages of the task and the procedures required for achieving the required coordinated performance. Some 'externalisation' of the internal (cognitive) procedures used by experts could assist learning of what is being modelled. For example, the expert might verbalise their thinking—'the clutch has to be smoothly depressed, but make sure to keep up the road speed, change gears quickly and then smooooooothly let out the clutch'; 'if the gauge comes up too quickly it means that . . .'; 'what I am considering at this point is . . .' In these ways, observation of the modelled performance and the experts' verbalisations permits learners to understand the goals for, and to attempt initial performances of, these tasks. For instance, the requirement to change gears using a gentle movement of the palm of the hand, rather than forcefully shifting the gear stick, can be made accessible through observation and experts' commentary.

Another important goal for modelling is making requirements for practice that are hidden from learners easier to understand. As shown later, workplace learning guides can use various strategies to ease the learning of knowledge that is not accessible by visual means alone. In addition, learners in workplaces have indirect access to other models, through observing and listening. These can allow learners to monitor their own performance and take an active role in identifying this kind of modelling and support.

Coaching

Coaching is a process of guiding and monitoring learning through work activities. Initial attempts at work tasks can be described as being immature approximations of the modelled tasks. As procedures are learnt and honed, these attempts increase the effectiveness of such approximations of the modelled tasks and become increasingly mature through these practices. That is, approximations of the task improve through practice and guidance so they become closer to the expert's smoothly performed and modeled procedures.

> Practice-orientated instruction's goal is . . . directed towards taking students through successive approximations of mature practice as they learn how to perform domain-specific tasks . . . This allows the learner to experience the full functional context of the domain. (Gott 1989: 98)

In coaching, strategies such as hints, feedback and clues, as well as demonstrations and modelling 'tricks of the trade', can be used to assist the development of the required workplace procedures. Coaching can include repeated demonstrations or remodelling of tasks, or parts of tasks, to assist learners improve their performance. The combination of practice and coaching assists compiling procedures, linking them into smooth productions. Providing supportive comments is part of coaching. These comments can encourage, maintain and direct the effort towards these activities. Coaching can be focused on specific tasks or more general requirements for work performance. At a specific level, guidance could be used to refine specific procedures. Taking the example of keyboarding. Novices could be coached first in placing the fingers on the keys without having to look down at them, then in using the 'shift' key to achieve a wider range of keyboard-controlled functions. Next, achieving improvements in the accuracy and speed of keyboard functions is practised. In seeking to develop more general problem-solving procedures, the car mechanic might coach the novice on how to diagnose a fault in a motor car. This might involve a procedure with the electrical system (e.g. see if a spark is being generated by the spark plug and alternator, then work 'backwards'; checking for mechanical faults starting with the fuel system). Coaching of this kind might be followed by coaching to assist understanding of each key component and links to the overall operation of the vehicle. A guide might also help coach a mechanic to understand how to set ignition points, or suggest some approaches to removing a bolt whose head has sheared. These examples illustrate the different goals for coaching in assisting initial learning.

Another role of coaching is to explain things that the learner is unable to experience or understand. For instance, a set of very dirty spark plugs might be taken as the reason a car's ignition system is faltering. However, a more experienced mechanic might suggest testing for a faulty condenser, which may be the cause of the dirty spark plugs and which would quickly cause the same problem with a new set of spark plugs. So coaching can help the learner to arrive at a level of understanding that would be difficult to achieve when other opportunities to develop it are absent.

Scaffolding and fading

Beyond initial modelling and coaching, ongoing support and monitoring can be provided in the form of *scaffolding*. This comprises providing learners with opportunities to practise independently those task for which they are ready while monitoring their performance with task performance. As Brown and Palinscar (1989: 411) state, the 'metaphor of a scaffold captures the idea of an adjustable and temporary support that can be removed when no longer necessary'. Freed from the need to monitor and coach closely, scaffolding supports the improvement in the learner's performance through guided practice. Support might be provided through suggestions, clues or assistance such as general reminders like: 'Why should you always start at the centre back and measure down from there and then move down from the chest to the waist and hips?' Scaffolding may involve carrying out part of a task that the learner cannot yet perform independently, or repeating modelling, or re-demonstrating the task. Scaffolding is premised on a collaborative approach to learning, with the learner taking the responsibility (i.e. doing the thinking and acting) for the work task. A requisite for scaffolding is an appraisal of the learner's readiness: their current skill level and the comparative difficulty of the work task they are to practise. *Fading* consists of the gradual removal of support until learners can independently perform the task proficiently. The indirect forms of guidance available in the workplace directly support this independent practice, as discussed in Chapter 3.

The duration and intensity of the phases of modelling, coaching, scaffolding and fading will differ according to learners' readiness and the demands of the task to be learnt. These strategies may tend to emphasise the development of procedures rather than conceptual knowledge. This is because much of the focus is on actual performance rather than the understanding required for performance. However, an important component of guided learning is the selected use of strategies aimed at developing understanding about vocational practice.

Strategies for developing understanding

The literature on learning through everyday work activity draws attention to the difficulties learners have in developing rich understanding through work. As discussed in earlier chapters, a rich understanding about the vocational practice is central to workplace performance. Berryman (1993) notes the growing significance of symbolic and other forms of conceptual knowledge in contemporary and emerging work practice. Referred to as being *opaque* or *hidden*, this knowledge may not be readily learnt because it is inaccessible for learners. For example, construction workers and miners need to understand concepts of force, pressure and load. Food workers have to know about hygiene and food contamination, even though many aspects of these concepts may remain hidden. However, these understandings are not always readily learnt through everyday work activities.

Although modelling and coaching can secure some of these outcomes, a number of strategies that specifically focus on conceptual development have been identified (Le Fevre et al. 1993; Pea 1993; Smith et al. 1993) and trialled (Billett et al. 1998; Billett & Rose 1999). Their selection is based on their usefulness for developing understanding and an ability to be used during everyday work activities. These strategies are:

- questioning dialogues;
- diagrams and models; and
- analogies.

Questioning dialogues
Questioning dialogues are interactions between experts and learners conducted through questions. They engage learners in a process of learning through successive phases of questions and responses. This process requires learners to elaborate, justify and substantiate their thinking, thereby extending it (Brown & Palinscar 1989). In the busy everyday world of work, it is tempting to simply tell, rather than to question. However, turning a statement into a question is an effective instructional process. An example of telling is: 'Next, we need to check the level of the water content before starting the extruder.' This directive could be turned into a question: 'What should we do before starting the extruder?' and/or 'Should we check the water content level now or later?' and 'Why?' As illustrated, these dialogues can involve both open and closed questions. Questioning dialogues usually comprise three successive stages:

- the learner constructing an explanation in their own words (explanation) in response to a question;
- clarification of explanation by learner (clarification); and
- exploring possible contradictions of initial conceptions (probing).

The guide's role is to:

- ask questions;
- seek clarification; and
- probe to test for and extend understanding.

The learners' tasks are to:

- provide an explanation (outlines their understanding);
- respond by clarifying (tests/extends understanding); and
- respond to probing question (tests/extends understanding).

For example:

Q   What do you think good client service is? (explanation)
A   Explanation provided by learner ....
Q   So, is what you are saying . . .? (clarification) ....
A   Clarification provided by learner ....
Q   What happens if . . .? (probe) ....
A   Response provided by learner ....

Diagrams and models
Diagrams and models can be used to provide physical or symbolic representations of objects or processes that are difficult to explain or experience. Again, it is important that learners are engaged in the thinking and acting, with the expert worker providing guidance. The same sequence of explanation, clarification and probing is used. The diagram need only be basic enough to visually represent the objects or processes. For instance, a drawing in the dirt or on a dusty work surface may be as effective as a diagram drawn on a piece of paper. Diagrams can be used to understand production processes, such as flow of materials or products, or complex service requirements, such as layouts of warehouses or restaurants. Equally, some

objects or models might be arranged in particular ways to illustrate a process. For instance, an open cut coal miner once explained how he used a kindergarten sandpit to demonstrate the removal of overburden to a group of novice miners at a new mine site. In doing so, he explained a process and outcomes that would only otherwise have been understood when the open cut coal mine was operational and developing. As with questioning, the expert will make judgments about how best to proceed based on the learners' readiness. For instance, whether the experts or the learners draw the diagram will be determined by the readiness of the learners. The process of using diagrams or models might be as follows:

- drawing of the diagram (explanation);
- seeking an explanation of its use (clarification); then
- probing for understanding.

The learning guide's roles include:

- drawing diagram/ask questions;
- seeking clarification; and
- probing to test understanding and extend knowledge.

The learners' roles include:

- drawing diagram (outlines their understanding) or responding to questions;
- responding by clarifying (tests/extends understanding; and
- responding to probing question (tests/extends understanding).

For example, in considering how to organise a production line for today's production:

Q Today, we have three product mixes to process, but one is required at twice the amount of the other two. How would you arrange the lines?

A Learner draws production lines and provides explanations.

Q Why have you put the production lines in this particular format?

A   Learner provides clarification (perhaps involving preparation, cleaning, size of product).

Q   What would you do and why, if the third line ran short of product?

A   Learner responds to probing questions.

Analogies

Analogies are used to link something learners already know with concepts that need to be learnt. A situation or circumstance occurring outside the workplace can be used as a basis for illustrating something that happens in the workplace. Similarities and differences can be pointed out by using the analogy. For instance, the example of the flow of water along a garden hose pipe is often used to explain how electrical current flows, with kinks in hose pipes being used as analogies for resistors. This links something we know with an important concept required for electricians' practice. The analogy of 'putting the learner in the driver's seat'—that is, getting them to do the thinking and acting—is applicable to many of the strategies referred to in this chapter. Analogies can be used by the guide presenting the analogy and the learner being asked to identify and/ or describe similarities and differences between the analogy used and the target situation or task.

GUIDED LEARNING IN PRACTICE

The guided learning strategies described above were evaluated in a study involving five workplaces (Billett et al. 1998). The study comprised the preparation of workplace learning guides (mentors) to use these strategies in the workplace and the monitoring of their implementation over a six-month period in each of the five workplaces. The selected workplace sites were diverse in terms of functions, goals, organisational structure and size. They comprised:

- a large food-processing company;
- a public sector agency associated with social service provisions;
- a textile manufacturing company;

- a recently corporatised power distribution company; and
- a small retail business.

Evidence of the effectiveness of the strategies and of everyday learning was gathered using 'critical incident' techniques and interviews with both guides and learners. The findings reveal much about the effectiveness of these strategies and how they should be used in workplaces. Included are the perceptions of learning guides (mentors) about the strategies, the overall contributions of guided learning and predictions about future use. Collectively, these data report the effectiveness of the strategies and the kinds of preparation required for guided learning to proceed in the workplace. In overview, the mentors reported that the key contribution of guided learning was its impact on workers' learning. The need to tailor guided learning to the particular needs of the enterprises and individuals within them was proposed as a key area for development. This arose from differing needs being expressed by mentors at different enterprises, often based upon the mentors' readiness and the structure and organisation of the enterprise. These needs varied markedly across the enterprises. At one workplace, which had a history of workplace-based learning arrangements, mentors wanted greater sophistication in the guided learning techniques. They combined different techniques and integrated them until, in some instances, they were used as part of everyday practice in this workplace, as in the 'learning curriculum'. Conversely, in another workplace, where there was little history of in-house skill development, the appointed mentors had difficulties using the strategies; there was limited time for their use; and the mentors perceived themselves to be unprepared for their role. The outcomes from this workplace generally reflected these concerns.

Strategy use

Views about the contributions of each guided learning strategy were provided by the mentors. Table 5.1 provides a summary of the findings of the perceived utility and limitations of each strategy. In this table, the left-hand column identifies the strategy, the middle column provides summary statements about its utility, and statements about its limitations are provided in the right-hand column. The findings from the five workplaces have been summarised, with responses sequenced in descending order of frequency. Those at the top were reported most frequently across the five workplaces.

Modelling

Modelling was credited with developing rapport, getting learners involved in hands-on tasks, providing opportunities to witness both desirable and undesirable performance, and the ability to monitor learners' progress. In addition, the authenticity of the context for this approach to learning was well supported. The limitations of modelling were associated with its inappropriateness to some workplace tasks (technological applications), placing the learner in a passive role during the modelling process, the difficulty with isolated learners, and concerns that modelling was time-consuming. The frequency with which modelling was used was middle range, yet was weighted in terms of its utility. Mentors predicted that they would use modelling frequently in the future. Significantly, learners in those workplaces where modelling was most frequently used enjoyed high levels of conceptual development during the period of the workplace trials.

Coaching

Coaching was held to be useful in assisting learners to adjust to new tasks, instilling confidence in their ability to succeed and providing them with challenges. According to the mentors, the ability to review the learners' work, reinforce learning, the sharing of knowledge and collaborative development were all provided for both mentors and learners through coaching. Mentors reported difficulty in knowing when to best use coaching, its linkages to and relations between mentor and learner, and difficulties associated with learners who were remote. Coaching was widely used and rated highly by the mentors across the five enterprises. According to their predictions, they will continue to use it frequently. The emphasis on placing responsibility on learners is evident in these findings, as is the need for expert workers to be helped in understanding how to use coaching as a workplace strategy.

Table 5.1   Mentors' perceptions of guided learning strategies

Strategy	Utility	Limitation
Modelling	Developing rapport with learners and getting them involved	Inappropriate
	Assists understanding of task by learners	Time-consuming
	Useful for hands-on tasks	Difficult to model technological applications
	Observing both good and bad performance	Learner in passive role—has to be followed by task engagement
	Accessing real examples	Different locations of learner and guide
	Monitoring of tasks	
	Another approach to address different needs	
Coaching	Instils confidence and provides challenge	Knowing when best to use it
	Observing both good and bad performances	Can be time-consuming
	Happens anyway, good reinforcement and support	Requires sound relationships between mentor and learner
	Structure to share knowledge	Inappropriate if relationship is not well founded
	Mentors can do own work, learners can pace themselves	Knowing how best to use it
	Both mentor and learner learning	Distance causes access problems
	Trouble-shooting and review of work	
Questioning	Determining learners' needs, understanding, and progress	Could be threatening if used insensitively
	Learners do the thinking and contribute	Forgetting to use it
	Immediacy of response	Has to be based on trust
	Looking at options	Not always appropriate
	First part of instruction	Other strategies more appropriate

Analogies	Likely to be retained	Not always best strategy
	Descriptive image requiring consideration of what is to be explained	Requires lots of thought
	Makes learning relevant and explains complex ideas	Difficult to get the right analogy
	Some examples obvious	Meaning not always shared between mentor/learner
	Making comparisons	
Diagrams	Explaining things (flow charts, equipment workings)	Not always appropriate (policies and practices, team building)
	Provides strong mental image	Quality of drawing
	Provides quick understanding	Limited opportunity—separate offices
	Explain complex ideas	Simplicity and precision
	Inducting new employees	Takes too much time
	Provides an overview	
	Thought out on paper, involving learner with drawing and questioning	

Questioning

Questioning was valued by mentors for its ability to help them understand learners' needs, access current knowledge and monitor learners' progress. Some mentors also valued the immediacy of questioning in providing information quickly and in a focused way and through its ability to engage learners in knowledge-building tasks. Concerns about questioning emphasised the importance of relationships between mentors and learners. Without carefully use, this strategy could be perceived as threatening by some learners. This was particularly the case where there was uncertainty about the motives for its use. Hence questioning needs to be used demonstrably in the context of learning rather than evaluating learners' knowledge for other reasons. Of the strategies specifically intended to develop conceptual understanding (i.e. questioning, analogies and diagrams), questioning was by far the most frequently used. Moreover, of these three strategies, questioning was supported as being the most likely for predicted future use. Most mentor concerns about questioning dialogues were how to use them effectively and how they could be seen as an instructional rather than an interrogatory device. Here again, the issue of the preparedness of the experts to use this strategy was evident.

Analogies

As was their aim, analogies were able to provide helpful links for the learners, making the subject more relevant. They were also held to assist with the retention of what was being learnt. Also, analogies were reported as being helpful in explaining complex ideas. Their limitations included the amount of preparation required to develop appropriate analogies, as mentors found difficulty in using them spontaneously. Further, the intended shared meaning was not always realised. Learners made their own connections, not necessarily those the mentors intended. Analogies were not used as frequently as questioning: they had the second lowest frequency of use, although the frequency of their use varied across the workplaces. The factor most likely to explain this variation was the mentors' differing readiness to use this strategy. Interestingly, where it was used most frequently, the mentors were typically tertiary educated. This may suggest that such a background could assist strategy use. However, even at these sites, there was no universal endorsement of analogy use in the future. Therefore, their application may be limited to workplace guides able to use analogies and stories to make links between what the learner knows and the required learning.

Diagrams

Diagrams were perceived as being useful for explaining concepts and procedures, and offering accessible representations to learners. They were also credited with providing quick understandings of some things that would have taken longer to explain by other means. One mentor integrated other strategies and used the generation of the diagram as a basis for her learner's development. That is, the learner created the diagram and responded to questions in conjunction with other strategies. In combination, this type of approach (as long as it does not overwhelm the learner) is likely to be a useful basis for developing and extending understanding. The limitations of diagrams included their perceived lack of applicability to many workplace tasks (policies and practices, team-building), mentors' ability to produce physical representations (quality of diagram), the problem of isolation, placing learners in a passive role and the time required to develop diagrams. Variability in their applicability to situations was evident. In particular, they were used successfully for explaining and developing an understanding of flowcharts, computer-related tasks, organisational structures and workplace processes. Some of the limitations were contradicted by their reported utility. Some mentors used diagrams with greater effect than others. However, across the five workplaces, diagrams were reported as being the least used strategy. Despite this, mentors typically and surprisingly predicted their future use in workplace learning. This prediction suggests that, in selected circumstances, diagrams are perceived to have particular utility. Also, they may not be as intimidating to use as questioning or analogies. Therefore, although there are restrictions on their application, they were still rated as quite useful by the mentors.

Mentors' perceptions of the utility of guided learning

The mentors were also asked about the overall usefulness of guided learning at work and what improvements they recommended to enhance its utility. Table 5.2 presents the summarised responses, capturing the utility and limitations of, and suggested improvements for, the guided approach to learning in the workplace. Again, the table illustrates the aggregated data from the five work sites, with the responses sequenced in descending order with the most frequent responses at the top.

The respondents stated that guided learning was useful in the learning and development of both mentors and workplace learners. For the mentors, guided learning provided a structure and reason for learning, and presented opportunities to reflect on their practice and to interact with other workers for the purposes of their learning. The mentors also reported that guided learning engaged learners in activities that addressed motivational issues and provided an additional source of advice (learning). The need for thorough preparation, time

Table 5.2 Mentors' perceptions of guided learning

Utility of guided learning	Limitation of guided learning	Improvements required
Caused conscious, structured and reflective approach to learning at work	Difficult to use	Reinforcement of and follow up with strategies
Pressed learners into thinking for themselves and mentor to reflect on work practice	Remoteness inhibited strategies and access to expertise	Thorough preparation and tighter focusing of preparation
Provision of a wider range of strategies	Too busy and unprepared	Time available to do task
Provided an opportunity to motivate learners	Uncooperative learners	More flexibility with strategies
Provided other sources of advice for learners	Learners uneasy with process	Provision of a structured checklist for tasks
Assisted with inducting employees to workplace	Mainly used for induction purposes	Locating mentor and learners in same physical environment
Provided an opportunity to structure learning of workers	Thorough preparation and specific focus on application to mentors' area of work	Should be part of job description
		Timing of program and selection of those involved

to undertake the role of a learning guide, a requirement for monitoring and providing feedback on their performance all emerged as key suggestions for the successful implementation of guided learning.

The lack of workplace learners' involvement in the implementation of guided learning in the workplace was seen as detrimental to the learning process and its outcomes at some work sites. In one workplace, the lack of information led to some learners being suspicious about the aims of the workplace learning process. Both the mentors and the learners shared these concerns. Another limitation was the physical separation between the guide and learner that restricted opportunities for face-to-face meetings. Separations included working in different parts of the same workplace, being in the same location but on different shifts or being geographically separated. In addition, the timing of the program and selection of individuals for mentoring programs were held as being determinants of the quality of learning outcomes. None of the limitations focused on the quality of opportunities to learn. Instead, they revealed personal and organisational constraints. Views about improving guided learning included the more thorough preparation of workplace guides and the monitoring of their performance. Closing the distance between remote learners and their mentors was also held to be essential. The timing of mentoring was not always welcomed at particularly busy periods in production processes. However, its use in the induction of new employees or to coincide with changes in the workplace was supported.

Building on the reported strengths of the guided learning process, and addressing concerns and suggestions for improvement, it is proposed that:

- a more thorough preparation for guided learning is required that includes more tailoring to the particular requirements of the workplace;
- mentors' initial preparation as learning guides needs to be followed up by support and feedback on progress;
- work tasks need to be structured so that mentoring is part of the job, thereby legitimating the time expended on this task; and
- the learners should also be thoroughly briefed on the program.

Having gauged perceptions of the effectiveness of guided learning in these five enterprises, findings about the contributions to learning from each strategy are presented and discussed below. An issue identified above, and persisting in these findings, is the need for guided approaches to learning to be responsive to specific needs within each enterprise.

The effectiveness of guided learning outcomes

The findings of the critical incident interviews provide evidence of the contribution of guided learning strategies to the resolution of workplace tasks. As reported in Chapter 3, everyday experiences were consistently found to make greater contributions to learning than the guided learning strategies referred to above. This outcome was anticipated, given previous findings about the ongoing and rich contributions to learning at work of everyday workplace activities, other workers and the workplace environment (Billett 1993b, 1994a, 1995a; Billett & Rose 1999). Nevertheless, the guided learning strategies also contributed to and augmented the learning realised through everyday work activity. There is a strong relationship between the frequency of strategy use and the effectiveness of these strategies in addressing work-based problems. The findings also show a clear relationship between achieving conceptual change (developing understanding) and the frequency of strategy use (Billett et al. 1998). The number of conceptual links made in the learners' concept maps indicates that the development of understanding was increased for many of the learners who had frequent interactions with these strategies. Linkages of this kind are seen to be associated with conceptual development because depth of understanding is premised on the interconnectedness of individual units of conceptual knowledge (Groen & Patel 1988).

However, different levels of association between strategy use and conceptual development were reported across the five workplaces. The majority of those learners whose conceptual development did not appear to increase were restricted to one workplace. At this workplace, the use of strategies was reported as being less frequent than others. At the other workplaces, high levels of strategy use were typically associated with increases in the number of conceptual links. So there is evidence of a correlation between the frequency of strategy use and levels of conceptual development. Therefore, it seems that when these strategies are used, understanding is also increased in the workplace—which was, of course, the intention. The findings also indicated that, of the three strategies selected specifically for this task (questioning, diagrams and analogies), only questioning was widely valued for its utility and was correspondingly most frequently used. It seems that analogies and diagrams were not used as frequently. Again, this suggests that a thorough preparation is required for workplace guides. The findings suggest that one of the key shortcomings of learning through work—the development of understanding—may be able to be addressed at least in part through the more frequent use of these kinds of strategy at work.

Guided learning: Learners' perspectives

Views about the guided learning process, its limitations and areas for improvement were also gathered from the workplace learners. Their responses are summarised in Table 5.3. In overview, these learners propose that the effectiveness of the process is a product of its outcomes (e.g. ability to secure knowledge), its processes (e.g. approach to learning) and their integration with workplace activities. Similar findings have been reported elsewhere (e.g. Dymock 1997). Key outcomes declared by the learners were learning about the organisation, its procedures and the knowledge required for performance in the workplace. Hamilton and Hamilton (1997), as well as Stasz and Brewer (1999), have also noted broader learning outcomes arising from students' participation in work placements. These have included social and organisational competencies. Other outcomes arising from learners in the five enterprises included individuals learning more about their own potential and developing shared relationships in the workplace. Similar findings have been identified elsewhere (Harris et al. 1997). Learning processes most valued across the five enterprises include collaborative, one-on-one, problem-based learning supported by the guided learning processes. These processes involve learners being engaged in problem-solving in the workplace when responding to new tasks and challenges. The integration between guided learning and workplace activities was viewed by some as being complementary and as providing pathways for learning the knowledge required for their work.

The limitations of guided learning from the learners' perspective can be categorised similarly. Problems occurred when goals for learning and relationships between the guides and learners were not clear and when expectations of the learning tasks were unrealistic. Limitations associated with the processes of guided learning were difficulties in accessing, or changes in, mentors, or limitations in the role adopted by the mentors. In addition, failure to build a relationship

Table 5.3 Learners' perceptions of guided learning

Utility of guided learning	Limitations of guided learning	Improvements required
Induction into work tasks, learnt about the procedures and culture	Accessing mentors who have other demands	Setting aside regular times to meet and talk
Guidance and support	Lack of time to make it work	Clearly establish goals and expectations for process and involving learners
Shared problem-solving between mentor and learner	Greater pro-activity from mentor	Don't assign someone, provide access to available expertise
Mentor best source of available knowledge	Pace and scope of expectations unrealistic	Initial appraisal of learner's experiences
Problem-solving—how to go about, paths to follow, learning new aspects of job	Not had much contact with mentor	Mentor to have a repertoire of strategies and examples
Provided one-on-one learning	More than one mentor required	Some structure for use of strategies Make it available to all staff
Effective approaches to learning	Goals and relationships not clear	Mentoring tightly linked to everyday activities
Learnt about my limits, developed supportive relationships	Difficulty in establishing shared understanding	Appoint mentor at senior level to whom the learner is subordinate
Helped understand workplace requirements	Timing right for both mentor and learner	Mentor more experienced colleague, not boss
Being placed in the deep end by mentor, while being monitored	Not enough time to establish relationship	Mentors prepared to interact more supportively with learners
Access to important technological knowledge		Need to get around shift problems
Mentoring complements learning at work		Consciously develop a rapport between junior and senior workers

with mentors, which included the development of a shared understanding, was reported as inhibiting the quality of interactions
between learners and guides. From the learners' perspective, limits
on the time available to undertake the role and difficulty with contact
between mentors and learners were key shortcomings to the way that
guided learning had been implemented in their workplaces. Suggestions for improvements were quite diverse. They were also different
for each work site. For example, at the workplace with a history of
workplace training, suggestions were about further refinements to
guided learning. These were of quite a different order than those
from another site where structured skill development was unknown.
Comparatively, these sites might be thought of as having, in one case,
a strong preparedness for guided learning and, in the other, a lack of
readiness for guided learning in the workplace. Yet, even in the
former, there was evidence that guided learning was not always successful. Conversely, in the latter, there was evidence of successful
learning. In both cases, individual factors played an important role in
these outcomes. In the first situation, one learner resisted the best
efforts of the mentor. In the second case, a mentor worked hard and
consistently to guide learners. These efforts were appreciated by the
learners and were deemed to be effective, given the findings from
the critical incident interviews.

However, learners commonly shared some concerns that, taken
together, suggest the framework for a set of principles for the conduct
of guided learning at work. Both improvements and a need to clarify
goals and expectations for both mentors and learners were suggested.
Improvements recommended for the learning processes were directed towards:

- a more thorough preparation of mentors;
- structured and regular meeting times;
- improved access to mentors;
- more guidance in the most appropriate use of strategies;
- selection of mentor; and
- the conscious building of relationships between mentors and
  learners.

The need to tightly link everyday activities and guided learning is advocated. From these findings, both organisational and personal factors can be seen to play an important role in determining the efficacy of guided learning processes in these workplaces.

In sum, there were three consistent findings about the potential of guided learning in the workplace. First, associations were identified between strategy use and development of the learners' workplace knowledge, which are of the kinds required for expert performance. As with earlier studies, it was found that everyday participation in the workplace develops much of the knowledge required for workplace performance. However, when guided learning strategies (modelling, coaching, questioning, diagrams and analogies) were frequently used, there was evidence of a marked development of learners' conceptual knowledge (see Table 3.2). Associations between strategy use and the strengthening of the development of conceptual knowledge suggest that persistence in the use of these strategies is worthwhile. They also suggest that the development of deeper forms of conceptual knowledge, which is a key shortcoming of learning at work, may be overcome through the use of these strategies. That is, these strategies can supplement and augment the kinds of learning realised through everyday activities, particularly in developing conceptual knowledge.

Second, different patterns of strategy usage and views of the strengths and weaknesses across the five workplaces indicated different types of requirements for, and readiness to participate in, guided workplace learning. The five workplaces in this investigation had diverse goals, functions and organisational structures, making questionable any general prescription for learning in workplaces. Gladstone (1988, cited in Garvey 1994) captures this diversity by suggesting that mentoring is 'as variable as the organisation in which mentors and proteges find themselves, and as idiosyncratic as the people involved'. The diversity of work practices, tasks and work areas within enterprises means that processes such as modelling and guidance may need to be conceived quite differently across workplaces. These differences are, in part, a product of the appropriateness of these strategies to workplace tasks and the difficulty of their use, but also of the readiness of workplaces and employees to participate in guided learning at work.

Third, there were unintended but significant outcomes for some learners beyond the direct development of the knowledge required for performance. A number of mentors and learners themselves reported heightened self-worth and confidence as a result of involvement in the guided learning process. Several mentors noted this effect on the learners, and this outcome was found in workplaces without a history of any structured learning in the workplace. Some mentors themselves reported that the process of guiding the learning of others had resulted in them reflecting on their own vocational practice.

Fourth, both a thorough and rigorous preparation for the learning guides and a briefing of those who are being guided is warranted. Establishing and managing rigorous workplace learning arrangements also requires enterprise commitment, including the time and resources to prepare mentors. Without this preparation and support, it is unlikely that the skills and confidence required for the guidance learning role would be developed. The preparatory process should include opportunities for practice, understanding the principles involved, and then monitoring, reviewing and refining the application of mentoring in the workplace. In addition, the learners should be informed of the processes in which they are to participate.

Fifth, the findings of the investigation indicated the potential of guided learning at work. They supported earlier findings that everyday activities at work have the capacity to develop much of the requirements for workplace practice. Moreover, when guided learning strategies reach the stages of being talked about, shared with, discussed by and observed by other mentors, they are inclined to be richly integrated and used as part of the 'learning curriculum'. If guided learning can become part of everyday activity in the workplace, the combined contributions should become quite potent, as guided learning will augment the contributions from participation in work. However, distance and other kinds of isolation (e.g. shift work, physical separation) present challenges for an approach to learning founded upon close interpersonal interactions between expert and novice: these need to be considered more fully, and are discussed in Chapter 6.

GUIDED LEARNING FOR TRANSFER

As was outlined earlier, there is also a third level of guidance at work. It is concerned specifically with learning that will transfer beyond the workplace situation in which the knowledge was initially learnt. This transfer could be to respond to novel or non-routine workplace tasks arising in the workplace or to transfer existing practice to other workplaces. Therefore, rather than having a specific workplace focus, this level of guidance seeks to assist workers to transfer their knowledge more generally within their vocation. This is not to suggest that the approaches to guided learning already described in this chapter are unconcerned with transfer or strategic outcomes. These three levels of guidance are seen as being those which should occur synchronously and as part of everyday working activities. However, in the third level of guidance, there is a clear and deliberate focus on learning that seeks to overcome the constraints of learning in one setting and that might inhibit the development of transferable vocational knowledge. Accordingly, this level of guidance can be viewed as developing vocational expertise that is applicable to circumstances other than where the original learning occurred.

Extending vocational knowledge through guided learning

The key characteristics of this third level of guidance are that the strategies to be adopted place a deliberate emphasis on engaging learners to extend their vocational knowledge. The aim is to develop self-assessment, self-regulation and monitoring skills within their vocation. Central to achieving this goal is the need to generate what Piaget (1967) refers to as disequilibrium in the learner—to press workplace learners into recognising the incompleteness of their vocational knowledge in order to motivate them to extend it further. As Brown and Palinscar (1989: 389) propose, 'adaptive change is presumed to be fostered in situations that encourage dissatisfaction with the existing state of knowing'. Accordingly, a key concern is to engage learners in producing the questions, scenarios and solutions and then monitoring their responses. These processes aim to foster habits of self-assessment, self-regulation and self-monitoring associated with the vocation. The developmental goal is to construct richer procedures and concepts associated with individuals' vocational domains. These include the self-regulated approaches to active problem-solving mentioned above, and the abstraction of principles associated with vocational practice.

Coaching and scaffolding (described earlier) can be adopted for such purposes. This is quite consistent with the goals of developing transferable knowledge through guided learning, as proposed by Brown and Palinscar (1989) and Collins et al. (1989). For example, coaching can be used to extend learners' knowledge. Asking learners to consider where else they can use a particular procedure or suggesting changes in approach, given the different application of a procedure or process, can assist in developing a robust base of knowledge. For example: 'If you were packing a pallet with a new type of box what would you need to do?' In urging learners to propose means for proceeding and to predict the scope of the applicability of their knowledge, the guide may have to advise about misconceptions that are easily arrived at and predictions that are immature. Analogously, coaching can also serve to direct learners' attention to important strategic components of the task, in conjunction with questioning, and those that may be known about, but not considered—for example: 'What do you need to consider before completing that part of the task? How will what is done here influence the next phase of the job?' This type of coaching can encourage learners to engage in more strategic and self-regulated thinking.

Equally, questioning and diagrams can encourage learners to extend their knowledge and to abstract principled knowledge from particular instances. For example, questioning might be used to help the warehouse worker establish a set of principles about pallet-packing that can apply to different kinds of packing and preparation for transportation (e.g. determining the strongest position for box). From experiences in nursing in different kinds of hospital wards, questioning might be used to draw out a set of principles and practices for nursing (e.g. duty of care, diagnosis, ways of handling patients' needs). This abstraction can assist with further applications of this knowledge (transfer) to situations and circumstances that are different from those in which it was initially learnt. So the warehouse workers and the nurses can develop sets of canonical knowledge associated with their vocation that will assist them to practise in circumstances that are different to those in which they were learnt. Architects might use diagrams, for instance, to develop some general principles for designing houses and means by which the requirements for areas for living, sleeping, entertaining, cooking and personal hygiene might relate to one another. These principles can then be used as bases for considering different kinds of housing designs, which includes an understanding of variations from the norms associated with addressing particular kinds of housing needs. These processes are focused on developing and testing the potential for generalisation of concepts or procedures associated with the vocational practice.

Generalising from what has been learnt

Using a process of questioning, workplace learners can also be encouraged to predict the extent to which what they have learnt is applicable to other situations and circumstances. The aim here is to extend the learning by developing a richer account of its potential applicability to other situations. Importantly, this includes recognising the limits of its generalisability. Having learnt how to perform a particular task or skill, workplace learners can be encouraged to understand the degree to which what they have learnt is more or less transferable to other situations—the limits of its application. They could also be asked where else the learning could be applied; what else it might be applied to, and be asked to identify the limits on the application of the learning. For instance, having learnt to thicken sauces using a roux, apprentice chefs could be asked to consider other applications for this technique of thickening. Then they could be asked to identify where it would not be appropriate. Hence the appropriateness of other techniques (e.g. the use of cornflour, arrowroot or cream) to these circumstances might be considered, with an emphasis on determining the circumstances where these would best be used. From such experiences, principles can be abstracted about how sauces can best be thickened and under what circumstances particular techniques are most useful.

One means of achieving generalisation of what has been learnt is for learners to experience how vocational procedures and concepts, and the values that underpin them, are manifested in different workplace settings. References have already been made to nurses coming to understand how nursing is manifested in different and similar ways across wards and units in hospitals. This is likely to result in the learning of procedures and understandings that can assist the transfer of nursing knowledge to other situations (e.g. different nursing workplaces such as community and workplace clinics) and circumstances (e.g. new and complicated medical procedures) through enriching the repertoire of nurses' experiences. Opportunities for learners to access different circumstances in which the vocational practice applies should be utilised if at all possible. Some apprenticeship systems provide these kinds of experiences. For instance, in some cookery apprenticeships, the apprentice might work in the banquet kitchens, go on to cook individually prepared meals in the restaurant and then work in the bistro of the same hotel. Later, they may work in a city restaurant, hospital kitchen or workplace canteen. As long as there is sufficient time to learn and reinforce what is learnt and understand differences between them, these diverse experiences may help to develop a rich and transferable body of vocational knowledge. So, if and where possible, work experiences should be structured to assist the development of transferable vocational knowledge, based on the development of the generalisability of the vocational principles and practices.

Self-assessment and comparisons with other workers

The monitoring and self-assessment of completed tasks is an important quality of expert performance (Stevenson 1994). Engendering this kind of habit plays an important role in developing self-regulated learning and assisting monitoring of the accomplishment of tasks. This can be achieved through encouraging comparisons in performance with other coworkers and experts. Schoenfeld (1985) refers to this as 'post-mortem analysis': reflection on completed tasks to consider and develop strategies for performance. From this reflection, the capacity for self-correction skills can be developed. This is an important component of self-regulated learning and of the development of knowledge robust enough to transfer to other situations.

Environments that 'encourage questioning, evaluating, criticising and generally worrying knowledge, taking it as an object of thought, are believed to be fruitful breeding grounds for the restructuring of knowledge' (Brown & Palinscar 1989: 395), as just outlined. There is potential for such environments to be created in workplaces. Through the use of questioning, getting learners to predict consequences and illuminating the breadth of applications, coworkers can assist in this development. Moreover, through the provision of experiences that grant access to some of the diversity of the vocation practice and its goals, robust outcomes may be generated. These arrangements offer the prospect of considerable returns to enterprises. Workers with sufficiently robust knowledge to deal with novel tasks arising from an ever-changing work environment should be an important asset. Further, the more vocational practitioners develop an understanding, the less they need to continually learn. Instead, the robust knowledge of experts—comprised, as it is, of rich understanding and well-honed procedures—is able to respond to change without the need for continual renewal of learning. Doctors' knowledge of physiology, for instance, permits them to understand changes in therapies and the likely ·impact of those therapies on particular conditions or series of conditions. They do not have to keep relearning each time a new therapy becomes available.

SUMMARY

Guided learning plays a central role in developing vocational knowledge in the workplace. It is an essential component of the workplace curriculum and any pedagogy for the workplace. The particular requirements of enterprises—and, indeed, of individual work areas within enterprises—mean that guided learning will be manifested in different ways across and within enterprises. Therefore, approaches to guided learning will be shaped by the characteristics of each workplace. Nevertheless, the evidence presented above indicates, in various ways, that guided learning helps to develop the kinds of knowledge required for work performance. That is, when the strategies are used frequently, there is evidence of the development of the kinds of knowledge required for workplace performance. Moreover, as expert workers become more skilful with guided learning strategies, their use may well become more integrated with the contributions of everyday work activities. Having said that, there will always be circumstances where direct guidance by more experienced coworkers may be difficult, and where other approaches—or variations on the approaches referred to here—become warranted. One of these situations is where workers are physically separated or geographically isolated. Many of those who need guidance are in situations where they work apart from those who can provide guidance. Also, conditions in workplaces might not always be conducive to direct interactions between workers while they are working. Noise, heat or the need for safety clothing can make direct interactions between the expert and learner difficult. For instance, with welding, the confined nature of the work, the noise and the level of eye protection mean that it is very difficult for interactions to take place. In such situations, consideration needs to be given to how learners and their guides are best able to interact. Adaptations to strategies such as the use of the telephone or electronic communication for workers who are isolated, or using times and places within the workplace where close guidance can be undertaken free from noise, heat and the encumbrances of safety attire, could be considered.

Notwithstanding these concerns, factors likely to underpin the successful implementation of guided learning are as follows:

- Positive relationships between guides and learners are an important precondition for success that has consequences for the selection of and induction of both mentors and learners. Both mentors and learners have responsibilities to engage in interactions that enhance collaborative relationships.
- Clear goals and expectations are required for the guided learning

program, with both mentors and learners being informed about
and involved in the determination of outcomes.

- Learners' access to mentors is essential, through regular meetings, face-to-face encounters, or distant means such as telecommunications.
- Where the workplace's culture of practice is open and familiar with developmental processes such as mentoring, such processes are more likely to be successful than where these conditions are not present.
- A thorough preparation is required for workplace experts who are to act as guides in the three levels of guidance identified above. Also, those learners who are to be the objects of the learning arrangements need to be briefed on what to expect and on their roles, responsibilities and the likely benefits arising from their participation.

These issues are largely associated with the organisation and management of workplace learning experiences, which are taken up in the next chapter.

6

Organising and managing workplace learning

ENTERPRISES AND THE WORKPLACE CURRICULUM

The quality of vocational practice learnt at work, the effectiveness of the workplace curriculum and the way in which guided participation proceeds will largely be a product of their organisation and management within the enterprise. The preceding chapters have advanced a case for developing vocational expertise at work. It seems that some of the knowledge required for expertise can be learnt through everyday work activities—'just doing it'. However, the structuring of workplace learning experiences can extend and supplement the contributions of everyday activities. This structuring involves the development of a workplace curriculum and the provision of guided learning by experienced or expert workers. The potential of such arrangements is supported by a number of studies, whose findings have provided links between the provision of guided learning at work and the development of vocational expertise. Such potential is likely to be welcomed by individuals interested in learning about or developing further their vocational practice through work. For workers in many industry sectors, vocational practice cannot be learnt or developed further anywhere other than in the workplace. The workplace curriculum is likely to be most welcomed in these situations. More broadly, workers of all kinds are being asked to maintain the currency and quality of their vocational skills as expectations of lifelong learning are now being directed towards adults' vocational practice (Forrester et al. 1995). A key basis for this ongoing learning is to develop further vocational practice through work. Enterprises, too, should welcome the prospect of a workplace curriculum, given its potential to develop the practice of the workplace. Importantly, the kinds of outcomes likely to be realised through the workplace curriculum are those that enterprises need in order to maintain their competitiveness in a dynamic and uncertain economic environment. These include the capacity to adapt to change and to generate novel responses to emerging challenges. Engaging workers in the development and enactment of the workplace curriculum can generate the reciprocal workplace relations that, according to Rowden (1995, 1997), characterise enterprises that stand the test of time and grow. Moreover, the elements of the workplace curriculum as set out here address the requirements that enterprises demand of vocational education programs—that is, they are relevant, pertinent, accessible and relatively low in cost.

However, full realisation of the workplace curriculum will only be determined by individual enterprises' commitment to it. So what has to happen within enterprises for the benefits of learning at work to be available? As noted, factors determining the quality of learning in the workplace are mainly either organisational or individual. Organisational factors include the quality of guidance (i.e. its accessibility and availability) and access to a sequenced pathway of workplace activities. Individual factors include the willingness of experts to guide and of learners to engage in guided learning. Organisational factors are direct responsibilities of the enterprise, and some of the individual concerns can be eased by actions within the enterprise. That is, what happens within the work practice will likely have a direct impact on the quality of learning at work. Therefore, the support and sponsorship of the enterprise will influence—in some ways, strongly influence—the quality of learning within the workplace. However, in making this point, it is important to reiterate that the quality of learning is not solely the responsibility of the enterprise's management. Instead, it is shared across the enterprise. Enterprises can develop learning arrangements, provide opportunities, and support and ease the access for participation in developing vocational practice. However, the direction, strength and persistence of individuals' participation will also be key determinants. Both as learning guides and as learners, individuals determine the outcomes of how they engage in learning. As has been shown, committed learning guides and learners can make up for a poor workplace learning environment, and rich learning environments can be rendered poor by reluctant learners. The ideal is for the workplace to afford a rich learning experience through quality guided learning, and for workers to participate with effort and persistence in these experiences. This ideal provides a goal for the organisation and management of workplace learning.

It seems that the roles for enterprises in realising this goal are fourfold:

- support for the development and implementation of the workplace curriculum;
- tailoring the workplace curriculum to the enterprise's work practice;
- encouraging participation by both learners and those who will guide; and
- the thorough preparation of guides and briefing of learners.

Rather than offering tight prescriptions, the evidence from investigations of work-based learning is used to propose broadly how enterprises might manage and organise the workplace curriculum.

SUPPORT FOR GUIDED LEARNING IN THE WORKPLACE

Enterprises are often attracted to work-based learning because of the prospect of accessible, pertinent and cost-effective ways of developing the skills they need for effective work practice. Some skills are developed through learning as part of everyday work activities. However, as already discussed, there is a need to prepare for and organise the structuring of workplace experiences and guidance. Enterprises are doubtless attracted to the apparent cost effectiveness of workplace learning arrangements, and to the relevance of what is learnt. However, just situating learning arrangements in the workplace is not sufficient. The organisation of those experiences to achieve enterprises' stated goals of relevant learning is also required. Workers' access to the pathway of work activities of increasing complexity and accountability is part of work practice in many—perhaps most—workplaces. However, this access may need to be structured and consciously managed and supported in the workplace. Resources need to be allocated to identify the pathways of activities, to establish what knowledge is difficult to learn, and to ascertain what learning constitutes expertise in workplaces. In particular, research on change (e.g. McLaughlin & Marsh 1978; Fullan 1983, 1985) supports what Sefton (1993) has found: that the wider the involvement and the more collaborative the approach adopted in the workplace, the more likely it is that there will be acceptance of what is implemented. It is not so much who initiates change that is important. Rather, whether workers are allowed to participate in the process of developing a workplace curriculum will influence its acceptance and adoption—or, conversely, its rejection—by those in the workplace. So the wider the involvement and engagement in determining the pathways of activities and identifying the requirements for work, the more likely its acceptance in the workplace will be.

The thorough preparation of workplace learning guides and the briefing of those who will work with these guides requires sponsorship and support within the enterprise. The degree of preparation and support required will differ across workplaces, depending on the readiness of those involved, the work practices and the values within the workplace, its size and the homogeneity of its functions. Guided learning is also dependent on an environment conducive to securing interactions among workers and opportunities to learn. Therefore it may be necessary to improve interactions between learners and guides, particularly when workers are isolated physically or geographically. Securing these interactions should become an accepted part of work practice. For instance, the customary consideration for providing opportunities and practice in Japanese corporations (Dore & Sako 1989) could be adopted. Accordingly, an inherent part of normal work practice would be to provide opportunities for learning and refinement through workplace tasks as opportunities arise.

The key goal of enhanced participation will necessitate finding ways to encourage workers who are reluctant to participate, and to moderate their access to situations where they have opportunities to learn and practise. However, expectations need to be realistic. Not all workers will be able to move through the pathway to expert practice at a pace of their choosing. This movement will depend on opportunities for engagement and practice in these tasks and enterprise needs. This movement needs to be paced appropriately, as it takes time to develop work-related knowledge, even more for expertise.

So what are the prospects of these concerns being addressed in workplaces? A view from the human resource development perspective suggests that enterprises and workers have never needed each other more than they do now (Davis 1995). Key factors in enterprises' long-term survival are development of a high level of enterprise-specific skills and individual workers' engagement with the enterprise (Rowden 1995, 1997). Moreover, Sefton (1993) has demonstrated the high degree of satisfaction and levels of participation realised when workers are involved in the planning of training arrangements within the workplace. This all suggests that employers might do well to more fully gain the commitment of employees. Yet, despite what Rowden (1995, 1997) and Davis (1995) propose, it seems other agendas often threaten collaborative bases within workplaces. Emerging employment policies and practices are eroding the traditional relationship between the employer and employee (Kempernich et al. 1999). Contractual and contingent work is becoming increasingly common (Grubb 1996), and is undermining employer interest in sponsoring the skill development of employees. At the same time, such trends place workers in precarious situations within enterprises. Further, the changing emphasis on lifelong learning in many Western economies is placing responsibility on individuals to maintain and develop their skilfulness (Forrester et al. 1995). This provides a further disincentive for employer sponsorship of employees' development. Among other issues, this scenario raises an important concern about lifelong learning arrangements for sections of the workforce for whom there are no courses available to maintain or develop their vocational practice. In such employment situations, the options are further limited when the commitment by enterprises to developing vocational practice is reduced. Current evidence suggests that enterprise sponsorship of training is increasingly focusing on the 'non-vocational' aspects of work performance associated with new management practices (Smith et al. 2000).

The context for the commitment to and sponsorship of workplace-based learning is complex and problematic. However, the quality of this learning is premised on this commitment and support. Moreover, the sufficiency of this support may be necessary for the enterprise's future, particularly if claims such as those of Rowden (1995, 1997) and Davis (1995) are accepted. While enterprises are drawn to the accessibility, pertinence and apparent cost-effectiveness of workplace learning, it would be mistaken to believe that rich learning outcomes are achievable without sponsorship and support. It follows that, unless workplace learning is organised and supported, the rich opportunity to learn the knowledge for work within the workplace could be squandered.

DIFFERENT REQUIREMENTS FOR DIFFERENT WORKPLACES

The requirements for the workplace curriculum, and the ways in which it should best be organised, will differ across workplaces. The goals and requirements for learning in each workplace will differ, as discussed in Chapter 2. These differences cannot simply be explained in terms of being better or worse manifestations of the occupational practice; they are simply due to different requirements for performance at work. At one level, this difference can be associated with how vocational practice is manifested in work practice—that is, the 'technical' requirements of the work in a particular workplace, the scope of tasks and interactions with others, the particular values prized in the workplace, and whether the learning is focused on maintaining and developing existing practices or being transformed to meet the changing demands of work. Situational needs influence the organisational structures and cultures of practice in workplaces, making implementation of a uniform curriculum virtually impossible. There are also differences in how guided participation at work is likely to proceed. Depending on whether workers enjoy broader or restricted discretion, quite different outcomes are likely. Close interactions between guides and learners are not always easy to uphold—for instance, when workers are part-time, contingent or home-based. The uncertainty of the relationships between these workers and the enterprise may also complicate the process of guided learning interactions. There are also workers who are geographically or physically isolated. Therefore, rather than easy and uniform access to guided participation, issues associated with physical (different or separate workspace), time (different shifts) and geographical (remote) isolation need to be understood in considering the requirements for guided learning in a particular workplace.

Hence the curriculum for a particular workplace needs to take account of the kinds of procedures that are most likely to best meet its needs, including factors associated with access to activities and guidance. From the investigations of the enterprises referred to in earlier chapters and other studies, factors have been identified that can inform the development of workplace learning arrangements. In Table 6.1, these factors have been classified under: task factors, work practice factors and relationship factors. The purpose of this table is to illustrate the implications for the workplace curriculum arising from these factors, which can be categorised in terms of goals for learning and learning processes. These are elaborated below.

Task factors

The kinds of work being undertaken and the changing character of this work will determine the requirements for workplace activities and hence the bases for the workplace curriculum. Potentially, there will also be a changing focus on the goals and activities that comprise the workplace tasks. For instance, the enterprise may be going

Table 6.1   Organisational factors influencing workplace curriculum

Factors	Implications for the workplace curriculum
Task factors	
Work activities and goals	Appropriateness of strategies to work activities
Focus for development (e.g. induction, ongoing development or strategic change)	Identifying the goals for and most appropriate approaches to guided learning
Work practice factors	
Workplace culture	Acceptance of the mentoring process
Proximity between guide and learner (close or far)	Means of making interactions closer or more direct
Workplace organisation and goals	Identifying the key organisational goals that are aimed to be secured through guided learning
Relationships between managers/ owners and employees	Need to build relationships based more on collaboration and trust
Workplace arrangements (e.g. shift work, team work, separate work areas)	Organising for interactions to occur and time made available for these interactions
Time available for preparation and implementation	Adequate preparation for and support of guided learning within the organisation
Unit size (e.g. number of workers and the diversity of their needs)	Delineating different work areas, their homogeneity and identifying their needs
What knowledge needs to be learnt	The kinds of learning required, the degree to which that learning is routine or opaque, etc. and therefore the strategies to be used
Relationship factors	
Mentors' and learners' dispositions	Preparation of guides to include engendering trust, enthusiasm and overcoming reluctance to participate
Age and gender of guides and learners	Addressing discomfort with younger mentors or those of another gender
Readiness to participate	Consideration of the existing knowledge of learners and guides, and motivation for participation
Confidence to guide	Developing learning guides' skills and knowledge
Standing in the workplace	Considering whether mentors will be seen as being credible in the workplace

through a period of growth which requires developing new employees' skills for work tasks. Alternatively, the enterprise might be experiencing a reduction in its workforce which usually leads to the need for the fewer workers to conduct a wider range of activities—multi-skilling or cross-skilling. Consequently, an enterprise moving along this pathway of change will primarily be concerned with broadening the skilfulness of its existing workforce and attempting to secure transfer to new situations. A variation of this scenario is enterprises that are changing their productive or service processes through the use of emerging technology. Again, the goals here are different. The need could be to develop new understandings, to overcome concerns about new technologies and to assist in the learning of knowledge of a symbolic kind that might well be difficult to learn (Martin & Scribner 1991) or has been physically and conceptually remote from workers (e.g. Zuboff 1988). Accordingly, understanding the differences in learners' readiness and their goals for learning relates to a consideration of the work tasks that have to be learnt.

Work task factors influence the appropriateness and use of guided learning strategies and their sequencing. For example, a workplace may have production processes hidden within plant and equipment, which require the use of diagrams to make them accessible. However, diagrams may be less useful in the development of counselling or negotiation skills, which may be more suited to techniques such as analogies or questioning. Equally, the degree to which observable procedures such as physical tool use are required may determine the use of modelling and coaching. So the kinds of knowledge to be learnt and the goals for learning will determine the approach to guided learning adopted in the workplace. Therefore, it is necessary to consider a fit between the selected approaches to guided learning and the requirements of the knowledge of work to be learnt.

Work practice factors

Factors associated with the organisation of work, the culture or environment in the workplace and familiarity with skill development processes play a significant role in how workplace learning is likely to proceed. The organisation of work will determine how interactions occur in the workplace and how guided learning, as well as communication and interactions with other workers, can best proceed. Procedures such as modelling and coaching are unlikely to be uniform, with adaptations required when, for instance, guides and learners are on different shifts, or separated by distance and without direct communication. If teamwork is a key component of work practice, the goals and processes of learning will need to include focusing on the ability to work in a team situation and the use of collective approaches to learning. Again, there are variations in the concept of teams at work. For instance, some teams utilise a hierarchy—such as those in the cockpit of an airplane or in the dental surgery. These hierarchies are accepted as an important part of practice. Hence the hierarchy might be the premise for the guided learning interactions. Alternatively, shift teams might have an appointed leader or be self-managed. Also, workplace factors such as unit size or the degree of homogeneity will determine the breadth of the kinds of development to occur and how it might proceed. These factors again suggest differences in approaches to developing and implementing the workplace curriculum.

The values and norms that comprise the culture of the work practice will play a significant role in how, and under what conditions, the implementation of a workplace curriculum proceeds. In some workplaces, there is knowledge and acceptance of work-based learning. Hence gaining an acceptance of its purposes may not be necessary. In other workplaces, interactions between workers for the purposes of developing skills may be quite novel. Concerns for both the guides and workers will arise if the goals for proceeding with work-based learning are not widely understood. For example, questioning might be taken as being interrogatory rather than concerned with developing understanding.

However, other values-based concerns go deeper than familiarity with work-based learning. For instance, the degree of trust between management and the workforce, and among affiliations within the workforce, influence individuals' participation. As noted earlier, in the coal mining industry, safety training can be viewed as the employer passing on safety obligations to employees. On the other hand, supervisors, management and even workplace delegates are concerned about the quality of learning outcomes when participation by workers is wholly driven by pay increments (Billett 1995b), rather than concerns for safe and effective work practice. So the degree to which the workplace values and supports learning arrangements focused on developing expertise will determine how workplace learning is enacted. Associated with this support is the readiness of both the guides and other employees to engage in guided learning. Readiness includes workplace experts' ability and willingness to guide the learning of others and the degree to which the learners value these arrangements enough to participate in them. In this way, and considering the motivations mentioned above, readiness extends beyond the ability to incorporate the learners' dispositions or willingness to learn. In sum, work practice factors collectively play a significant role in determining how, and under what circumstances, the workplace curriculum will be conceptualised, developed, organised and managed in the workplace.

Relationship factors

Given the significance of interactions in guided participation at work, the quality of relationships among individuals in the workplace will also determine how the learning curriculum is enacted. Employees have a tendency to want to self-select the person who will guide their learning. However, the bases for self-selection differ. Some employees want supervisors to be their guides (sometimes in order to impress); others reject such guidance, because of the need to separate developmental and management roles. In some situations, supervisors lack the vocational competence to guide learning effectively (Billett et al. 1998). Other factors influencing the relationship between guides and learners include age and gender. Some workers find it difficult or even demeaning to be guided by somebody younger or whom they perceive to be of a lower status or an inferior gender. The standing of individuals in the workplace and their confidence to perform their role will influence this relationship. In the contested terrain of the workplace, individuals will enjoy different kinds of credibility with different individuals. For some people, some guides will never be acceptable, whether on the basis of personal histories, occupational affiliations or cultural practice. Importantly, such relationship matters are not wholly the responsibility of the expert or 'experienced other'. They are also the responsibility of the employee/learner.

So, given the shared process of learning, it is necessary to emphasise that both guides and learners have mutual responsibilities in their relationships and for their learning. It is true that workplace interactions often take place in conditions of unequal relationships. For many workers, the task of interacting with others to develop their skills will also be a challenge for which they may lack confidence. This can influence their willingness to participate.

In sum, factors associated with work activities and goals, the workplace culture and organisation and the relationships within the workplace will shape the form of the workplace curriculum in enterprises. It is these factors that will influence how the workplace curriculum is to be developed and enacted. The next section takes up the issues of encouraging participation through an environment conducive to a workplace curriculum and preparing those participating in guided learning.

ENCOURAGING PARTICIPATION

The studies of workplace learning found that, in the main, employees are willing to participate in work-based learning activities. However, there are differences in the form that this participation takes. One of the workers referred to in the vignette in Chapter 1, who actively set out to learn what others were doing, was so enthusiastic that the safety officer had to warn him not to enter areas that were out of bounds. On the other hand, there were workers whose reluctance stemmed from low levels of literacy or communication skills, or who would only engage in activities for which they received immediate remuneration. Some guides participated cautiously, as they found interacting with others and some of the strategies involved difficult. Because individuals regulate their own learning, grudging participation may lead to the intended learning being weakly appropriated (mastered). In particular, reluctance to engage in the kinds of demanding activities associated with learning new knowledge and reinforcing that knowledge will have consequences for those individuals' learning. Reluctance by experts to be partners in assisting learners' knowledge construction can also have detrimental effects. Not all workplace experts are willing to share their knowledge, particularly when they are concerned about displacement by those whom they have guided and supported (Lave & Wenger 1991). Experienced workers may be reluctant to show others how to do a particular task, if they believe it is against their interests or those of their affiliates. Secondly, workers may fear challenges to their status by those whom they are assisting to learn (Moore 1986). Given the uncertainty of contemporary employment practice, experts who are not rewarded or recognised for their contributions to others' learning and/or who fear displacement arising from their contributions will be reluctant to provide guidance and access to tasks if their own standing is threatened. As noted earlier, in Japanese corporations, because promotion is based on seniority, supervisors are willing to share their knowledge with subordinates and make arrangements for them to learn new tasks, confident of not being displaced by their subordinates (Dore & Sako 1989).

Individuals are also reluctant to participate effortfully in workplace learning when it is perceived as being largely directed towards the employers' interests. This includes concerns about transference of responsibility (Billett 1995b) or when programs are seen to be too enterprise specific (Billett & Hayes 1999). The workers in these studies were not confident that their best interests were always considered by enterprises in these programs of learning. When the content or focus of learning arrangements is perceived to be limiting the employees' prospects or is focused too closely on the enterprise's goals alone, it stands to be rejected or learnt only to the necessary level of mastery (Wertsch 1998). Therefore, it is perhaps shortsighted of employers to believe they can secure their employees' commitment in this way in programs where the content and outcomes are highly enterprise specific.

Consequently, means need to be identified and enacted for reassuring experienced workers that their efforts in guiding learners will not result in their displacement, marginalisation or replacement.

Without such means, their full contribution is unlikely to be forthcoming. Also, arrangements for engaging workers' interests and addressing their needs are required in developing workplace learning arrangements. These needs extend to providing robust preparation and development that can be formally recognised. Some countries have adopted wider certification models than those wholly premised on participation in formal education programs. The practice of using external examination bodies may assist in overcoming concerns about certification premised in the workplace; however, these require sponsorship. One clear requirement for the development of skills is for practice to occur over time. Workers who are only given some initial encounters and experiences and not allowed to develop fully the knowledge required to perform (i.e. to compile procedures and chunk concepts) may develop knowledge that is brittle rather than robust— that is, it will not transfer to new situation or circumstances. Hence expectations about access to and movement along the pathway of experiences have to be realistic, as the knowledge required for work will take time and practice to develop.

In conclusion, a collaborative approach to developing, implementing and monitoring the workplace curriculum may assist in overcoming reluctance to participate. As proposed in Chapter 4, there is a need to understand the requirements for and pathways towards full participation or expertise from both experienced workers and those 'newcomers' on the pathway. This kind of involvement eases acceptance of and participation in work-based learning (Sefton 1993). Further, a thorough preparation is required to overcome some of the concerns of experienced workers. Also, those who are to become learning guides will need to demonstrate particular attributes.

SELECTING THE GUIDES

The roles for learning guides were discussed in Chapters 4 and 5. In part, these comprise interactions between more experienced workers as guides and learners who are less experienced, as well as the use of strategies to develop procedures, concepts and dispositions required for performance at work. As noted, the most common practice is for enterprises to nominate a learning guide, usually a supervisor. Some—though not all—workers find this acceptable. Findings from the workplace studies suggest that workplace learning guides should:

- have expertise in the work area—be an expert other (can handle novel problems) and possess work-related knowledge to share with learners (must be viewed as being credible);
- understand the goals for performance—understand what is required for successful performance in the workplace;
- value guided learning—see a need for it and for the knowledge to be learnt by learners;
- have a willingness to share knowledge with learners; and
- be a guide for learners rather than a teacher (making learners do the thinking and acting).

These characteristics emphasise that a learning guide requires appropriate vocational expertise, and an ability and willingness to work collaboratively with workplace learners. One difference between facilitation of learning as referred to in other models of development such as 'action learning' or 'problem-based learning' and the model adopted here is that the guides are themselves a rich source of the knowledge to be shared with learners. An important role of the guides is to assist the learning through joint problem-solving with learners and other kinds of collaborative interactions. Therefore, beyond having expertise in the work area, guides also need to possess the ability and commitment to interact with and guide the learning of those who are less experienced and knowledgeable. More than someone merely facilitating learning, expertise is required to assist this learning through informed guidance.

PREPARING THE GUIDES

A thorough preparation for learning guides is essential to maximise the contributions of the workplace curriculum. In the study referred to in Chapter 5, despite some preparation, not all mentors found the strategies easy to use. The mentors consistently reported the need for a more thorough preparation than the half-day preparatory workshop and some supportive monitoring of their guidance in the workplace. In order to provide appropriate guidance, experienced workers need an understanding of and competence in the guided approach to learning to secure the desired learning outcomes in their learners, including a capacity to engender collaborative relations with coworkers. The amount of preparation required to achieve this goal will differ from enterprise to enterprise (Billett 1994a; Billett et al. 1998; Billett & Rose 1999). Differences are locatable in individuals' readiness to perform the role, the knowledge to be learnt in the particular workplace and the workplace's culture of work practice. Some individuals will require more preparation than others and some workplaces will present more formidable challenges to guided learning than others. Notwithstanding these differences, the preparation for guided learning has three dimensions. These are developing:

- an understanding of guided participation at work;
- an ability to use the guided approaches to learning and the techniques selected for use as part of everyday work activity; and
- the ability to build relationships.

Understanding guided learning at work

Understanding the principles of guided participation in the workplace is necessary for that guidance to be effective. These principles include learning through everyday goal-directed activities, the bases of individuals' construction of knowledge, being guided in learning rather than being taught, and the kinds of knowledge required for vocational expertise, including knowledge which is difficult to learn. The principles underpinning techniques such as coaching, modelling and scaffolding also need to be understood, as do the techniques focusing on developing conceptual knowledge. Furthermore, understanding the importance of building relations with learners to assist collaborative interactions is required. The preparation of the mentors in each of the five workplaces studied (Billett et al. 1998) used a prepared handbook, explanations and questioning to develop the mentors' understanding of the approaches to guided learning. The handbook was a resource later used as a reference when engaged in guided learning. In other situations, a summary of the techniques and a checklist for their enactment that fits onto one folded piece of paper that fits into workers' shirt pockets have been developed.

Guided learning methods and techniques

The procedural preparation should aim to develop the capacity to use the guided learning techniques as part of everyday work activities. This includes the ability to use these techniques in the workplace, understanding the circumstances in which they could best be applied in a particular workplace context, and understanding their selective use. This includes having the capacity to judge where each strategy is likely to be more or less effective. The preparation process needs to account for the differences that emerge in strategy use. As noted in Chapter 5, coaching and modelling were commonly reported as being easier to use and more applicable than the other three guided learning strategies. Of these strategies, questioning was used most. Both diagrams and analogies presented problems for some mentors and learners alike. Mentors reported that diagrams had quite specific utility, and were not widely applicable. Diagrams were seen to be useful in addressing knowledge associated with flow processes and procedures that were hidden from view. They were favoured in areas such as computer-based systems—for example, the steps involved in locating and using a program—and where production flow needed to be understood. Most, though not all, mentors also reported that analogies had proved to be problematic. Learners reported mentors earnestly trying to generate analogies as they engaged in mentoring. However, this hesitancy disrupted the interactions between learners and mentor.

The preparatory workshops for the mentors in the five enterprises studied (Billett et al. 1998) used modelling and coaching to initially demonstrate and develop the use of guided learning techniques. The participants were also asked to consider where each of these strategies could most appropriately be used in their area of work. They then practised the techniques with a peer, with another

individual monitoring and coaching the development of the procedures. However, these half-day workshops proved inadequate for the
preparation of workplace guides. Clearly, longer periods of time are
required to develop these procedures and support their introduction
in the workplace setting. In a recent project, two half-day sessions
were used. The first established understandings about the use of the
techniques, while the second practised and developed those techniques further. Much of this practice occurred in the workplace itself.
Further, initial monitoring and support in the workplace for use of
the strategy by a more experienced learning guide were commonly
proposed as a means to improve the development of the learning
guides' ability to perform these activities well.

Building relationships

The quality of relationships between guides and learners is also
central to learning outcomes. As guided learning is based on interpersonal interactions, engendering positive collaborative relations is
important. Learning guides need to balance encouraging learners to
do the thinking and acting, without them believing that they are 'on
trial' and without making the task too difficult. The use of supportive
comments may help build relations. Common understandings of such
issues as the expectations of the relationship, and initiating and maintaining contact, are needed in order for the relationship to flourish.
Those being prepared as learning guides need to consider the importance of being empathetic, postponing judgment, providing supportive feedback and seeking to develop a relationship focused on
developing workers' knowledge.

Therefore, preparation for guided learning needs to go beyond
understanding techniques and initial training in their use. It also
needs to provide guidance about how the collaborative relationships
can best be developed, including discussion of the roles, responsibilities and expectations of mentors and learners. Monitoring of
mentors' progress, provision of feedback and advice for refinements
are also likely to provide the kind of ongoing developmental opportunities required for developing guided learning at work.

PREPARING WORKERS/LEARNERS

In order to enhance involvement and overcome potential concerns about the workplace learning process, all learners to be involved in the workplace curriculum should be briefed about the aims of the guided learning and the processes being used. The briefing might comprise an overview of the kinds of learning outcomes being attempted, the goals for this learning, the kinds of guided learning techniques they are likely to encounter and the role of the learning guides. If the goals for learning relate to extending knowledge, accessing new ways of working, using new technologies or widening the scope of work tasks, then it is necessary to emphasise these goals. If an understanding of the goals can be generated, together with some involvement in the development of the workplace curriculum, participation probably will be more full bodied. First, the workers' responsibilities as learners need to be clearly stated, together with the probable outcomes and benefits they will gain from participation in the guided learning. This briefing could also be used to explain that the aim of guided learning is to get the learners to do the thinking. Second, it should be emphasised that the learners are not being appraised for any purpose other than their development. That is, strategies such as questioning are not intended to interrogate, but to extend their learning. However, achieving this may only take place through the demonstration of good practice. Third, expectations of the learning guides should be clearly stated. Fourth, if there is a need for any inducement, rewards or certification from participation, this needs to be clearly articulated. In many instances, there will be industrial concerns that focus on matters of pay, progression and certification, and these need to be addressed in the early stages.

EXTERNAL ASSISTANCE

The development of a workplace curriculum and the preparation of learning guides can be quite demanding. Clearly there is considerable work involved in identifying and tailoring the workplace curriculum and guided learning to address the needs of each workplace.

Depending on the enterprise's readiness, external assistance might be required to assist with developing these arrangements and establishing, managing and monitoring the guided learning process until the capability to undertake these tasks has been developed within the enterprise. The assistance of consultants or teachers might therefore be sought to develop and implement the workplace curriculum. However, such assistance needs to be enacted in ways that are consistent with conceptions of the workplace as a learning environment with its own characteristics, strengths and weaknesses. In many instances, workplace-based learning arrangements have been established using a classroom-based pedagogy, rather than one best suited to the workplace. Therefore, any external assistance used for these purposes needs to be mindful of the requirements and the contributions of guided participation in workplace activities, rather than being premised on the interactions and processes of educational institutions and uncritically applied to workplaces.

SUMMARY

In sum, a workplace curriculum has much to offer enterprises and those who are employed within them. However, the quality of those provisions will be determined, in large part, by how enterprises support the management and organisation of the workplace learning arrangements. Four broad roles have been identified for the organisation and management of the workplace learning curriculum in enterprises. First, learners' access to activities and guidance is central to the quality of learning experiences at work. To best utilise their potential, these experiences need to be organised into pathways of activities, supported by guided participation to develop the knowledge required for workplace performance and more strategic outcomes. Enterprise support for and sponsorship of these arrangements are necessary to achieve these outcomes. Second, each workplace will have unique requirements in terms of its goals for learning and preparedness. These requirements extend beyond the technical aspects of vocational practice and include the organisational factors and relations that shape the workplace curriculum, its development, and requirements for implementation and maintenance. Enterprise support is a precondition for the development of such arrangements, together with any development of collaborative arrangements and the environment required for their successful implementation. Third, encouraging participation in the workplace curriculum by both those who guide and those designated as learners is a central concern. The presence of contestation in workplaces—conflicts between individuals and groups—is sometimes beyond the scope of the workplace curriculum or the enterprise to resolve. However, considered and collaborative action in the development and implementation of the workplace curriculum may overcome some of the reluctance of guides and workers to participate fully in workplace learning. Fourth, the thorough preparation of learning guides and a briefing of those involved as learners regarding the purposes, process and outcomes of their involvement are required. The kind and degree of preparation needed for the workplace curriculum will differ across workplaces. These differences should be reflected in the kinds of knowledge to be learnt and the readiness for guided learning in the workplace.

This book has attempted to legitimise workplaces as learning environments and to propose how they might be used to effectively develop vocational expertise. It has been necessary to emphasise and build upon the contributions to learning that arise from everyday thinking and acting in the workplace. In proposing the rich contribution of the workplace to learning, an account of differences between the practices of educational institutions and those of workplaces has been required. Drawing on the particular set of attributes that workplaces provide, and the differences that mark learning in workplaces from that in educational institutions, a pedagogy for the workplace has been proposed. The central and interrelated propositions of this pedagogy are a workplace curriculum and guided learning at work. The workplace curriculum is seen as complementary to conceptions of curriculum adopted for educational institutions, although it has been structured to reflect the pedagogical practices most appropriate to workplaces. The use of guided participation at work is advanced as the other key pedagogic practice that reflects current thinking about how learning for the development of vocational expertise might be developed. However, it is the ability to enact this pedagogy in workplaces that will ultimately determine its usefulness or otherwise. There are clear beneficial outcomes arising from the workplace curriculum for both individuals and enterprises. Ultimately, whether these outcomes will be realised is dependent on the support for, and organisation and management of, these practices in the workplace and the ways in which individuals engage in such guided activities.

APPENDIX 1: ITEMS TO IDENTIFY THE PATHWAY FROM PERIPHERAL TO FULL PARTICIPATION

Questions that might be asked in determining the pathway of activities

- What is the range of tasks undertaken here on a normal work day?
- What is the range of activities undertaken in a busy period?
- What are the activities you only conduct weekly?
- What are the activities you only conduct infrequently (perhaps monthly or yearly)?
- What are the activities you conduct only occasionally but which are important for your work?
- What activities are only undertaken by experts?
- What is the sequence of work activities that new workers learn about on the pathway to being an expert in the work area?
- What is the sequence of tasks that novices should ideally learn on their way to becoming an expert?

APPENDIX 2: ACTIVITIES IN THE SALON—WHO DOES WHAT?

Could you please indicate who does which activities in the salon by placing a tick in the boxes. Please provide comments where appropriate.

Unit	Description of activity unit	Normally done by					Comments
		Qualified hairdresser	1st year apprentice	2nd year apprentice	3rd year apprentice	4th year apprentice	
1.1	Comply with health regulations						
1.2	Provide a relaxed and caring environment						
1.3	Prepare and maintain work area						
1.4	Check and maintain tools and equipment						
1.5	Check and maintain stock						
1.6	Apply occupational health and safety principles						
2.1	Follow routine instructions and information						
2.2	Participate in work groups and teams						
2.3	Apply professional ethics						
2.4	Support the organisation						
2.5	Receive and refer customer complaints						
3.1	Schedule, receive and direct clients						
3.2	Answer the telephone						
3.3	Complete client details						
4.1	Gown and protect clients						
4.2	Shampoo hair						

APPENDIX 3: IDENTIFYING THE LEARNING PATH-WAYS AND TASKS THAT ARE DIFFICULT TO LEARN (an example from a manufacturing plant)

Extraction area

	Learning sequence	Difficulty to learn
Preflight check		
Start up		
Running/operation		
Shut down		
Vacuum transfer system		
GMP check/set up		
Loading pallecons		
Cleaning pallecons		
Changing pallecons		
Cleaning pallecon tipper		
Cleaning hold silo		
Liquid additives		
Check list mono pumps		
Liquid feed rate check		
Shut down		
Liquid feed calibration		
Raw materials		
Production plan check		
Ordering		
Storage		
Fruit paste		
GMP check		
Turn on hot water system		
Production plan check		
Paste skid connection for line A & B		
Connection & position of pumps		
Changing of drums/purging		
Running extractor		

Cleaning extractor during production		
Vacuum bag lifter		
Pigging out the line		
Cleaning		
Turning off hot water service		
Disconnecting skid		
Shutting down pumps		
End of production		
Cleaning of drums		

1   Indicate numerically in the first column (learning sequence) how you would sequence learners' undertaking the tasks you have identified (place number 1 against the task they should learn first, 2 against the task they should learn second, etc.).

2   Using the listing as a prompt, identify what you believe to be the critical skills and knowledge required for work in this work area.

3a Which of the tasks you identified are particularly difficult to learn? In the second column (difficulty to learn), place a star or stars to indicate tasks that are difficult to learn.

3b Provide some examples of why these are difficult to learn.

4a List the ways individuals in the workplace currently learn the skills and knowledge required for work practice.

4b How do workers currently learn these 'hard-to-learn' skills?

5   What skills and knowledge do you need to link the activities across the four work areas?

6   In addition to what you have already provided, what knowledge do you need to learn, yet may never actually have to use in your work (e.g. safety fire exits)?

Thank you for your participation.

References

Alexander, P.A. & Judy, J.E. 1988 'The interaction of domain specific and strategic knowledge in academic performance' *Review of Educational Research* vol. 58 no. 4, pp. 375–404

Anderson, J.R. 1982 'Acquisition of cognitive skill' *Psychological Review* vol. 89 no. 4, pp. 369–406

—— 1993 'Problem solving and learning' *American Psychologist* vol. 48 no. 1, pp. 35–44

Anderson, J.R., Reder, L.M. & Simon, H.A. 1996 'Situated learning and education' *Educational Researcher*, May 1996, pp. 5–11

Bailey, T. 1993 'Organizational innovation in the apparel industry' *Industrial Relations*, vol. 32 no. 1, pp. 30–48

Ballenden, C. 1996 *Swings and Roundabouts—The Experience of Implementing a Work Based Traineeship*, vol. 2 of the proceedings of Learning and Work: The Challenges—4th Annual International Conference on Post-Compulsory Education and Training, pp. 61–70

Barley, S.R. & Orr, J.E. 1997 'Introduction' *The Neglected Workforce*

Between Craft and Science: Technical Work in U.S. Settings eds S.R. Barley & J.E. Orr, Cornell University Press, Ithaca NY, pp. 1–19

Bereiter, C. & Scardamalia, M. 1987 *The Psychology of Written Composition*, Lawrence Erlbaum & Associates, Hillsdale, NJ

—— 1989 'Intentional learning as a goal of Instruction' *Knowing, Learning and Instruction, Essays in Honour of Robert Glaser* ed. L.B. Resnick, Lawrence Erlbaum & Associates, Hillsdale, NJ, pp. 361–92

Bernhardt, A. 1999 *The Future of Low-wage Jobs: Case Studies in the Retail Industry* Institute on Education and the Economy Working Paper No. 10, March 1999, Columbia University, New York

Berryman, S. 1993 'Learning for the workplace' *Review of Research in Education*, vol. 19, pp. 343–401

Bertrand, O. & Noyelle, T. 1988 *Human Resources and Corporate Strategy: Technological Change in Banks and Insurance Companies in Five OECD Countries* Organisation for Economic Co-operation and Development, Paris

Bijou, S.W. 1990 'History and educational applications of behaviouralism' *The Encyclopedia of Human Development and Education Theory, Research, and Studies*, ed. R.M. Thomas, Pergamon Press, Oxford

Billett, S. 1993a 'What's in a setting—learning in the workplace' *Australian Journal of Adult and Community Education* vol. 33 no. 1, pp. 4–14

—— 1993b 'Authenticity and a culture of work practice' *Australian and New Zealand Journal of Vocational Education Research* vol. 2 no. 1, pp. 1–29

—— 1994a 'Authenticity in workplace learning settings' in *Cognition at Work: the Development of Vocational Expertise* ed. J.C. Stevenson, National Centre for Vocational Education Research, Adelaide, pp. 36–75

—— 1994b 'Situated learning—a workplace experience' *Australian Journal of Adult and Community Education* vol. 34 no. 2, pp. 112–30

——1994c *Evaluating Modes of Skill Acquisition* Centre for Skill Formation Research and Development, Griffith University, Brisbane

—— 1995a Structuring Knowledge Through Authentic Activities, unpublished PhD dissertation, Griffith University, Brisbane

——1995b *Skill Formation in Three Central Queensland Coalmines: Reflections on Implementation and Prospects for the Future* Centre for Research into Employment and Work, Griffith University, Brisbane

—— 1996a 'Constructing vocational knowledge: History, communities and individuals' *Journal of Vocational Education* vol. 48 no. 2, pp. 141–54

—— 1996b 'Towards a model of workplace learning: The learning curriculum' *Studies in Continuing Education* vol. 18 no. 1, pp. 43–58

—— 1998 'Understanding workplace learning: Cognitive and sociocultural' *Current Issues and New Agendas in Workplace Learning Perspectives* ed. D. Boud, National Centre for Vocational Education Research, Adelaide, pp. 47–68

—— 1999a *Changing Work, Practices and Engagement: Understanding Performance at Work* Faculty of Education, Griffith University, Brisbane

—— 1999b 'Experts' ways of knowing' *Australian Vocational Education Review*, vol. 6(2), pp. 25–36

Billett, S. & Hayes S. 1999 *Meeting the Demand: The Needs of VET Clients* National Centre for Vocational Education Research, Adelaide

Billett, S., McCann, A. & Scott, K. 1998 *Workplace Mentoring: Organising and Managing Effective Practice* Centre for Learning and Work Research, Griffith University

Billett, S. & Rose J. 1999 'Securing conceptual knowledge in the workplace' in *Learners' Learning and Assessment* ed. P. Murphy, Sage Publications, London, pp. 329–44

Boud, D. 1998 'A new focus on workplace learning research' *Current Issues and New Agendas in Workplace Learning* ed. D. Boud, National Centre for Vocational Educational Research, Adelaide

Boud, D. & Garrick, J. 1999 'Understanding workplace learning' *Understanding Learning at Work* eds D. Boud & J. Garrick, Routledge, London, pp. 1–12

Brown, A.L. & Palinscar, A.M. 1989 'Guided, cooperative learning and individual knowledge acquisition' *Knowing, Learning and Instruction: Essays in Honour of Robert Glaser* ed. L.B. Resnick, Lawrence Erlbaum & Associates, Hillsdale, NJ, pp. 393–451

Brown, J.S., Collins, A. & Duguid, P. 1989 'Situated cognition and
✝   the culture of learning' *Educational Researcher* vol. 18 no. 1,
     pp. 32–4
Butler, E. 1999 'Technologising equity: The politics and practices of
     work-related learning' *Understanding Learning at Work* eds
     D. Boud & J. Garrick, Routledge, London, pp. 132–50
Candy, P. & Mathews, J. 1998 'Fusing learning and work: Changing
     conceptions of workplace learning' *Current Issues and New Agendas
     in Workplace Learning* ed. D. Boud, National Centre for
     Vocational Education Research, Adelaide, pp. 9–30
Casey, C. 1999 'The changing contexts of work' *Understanding
     Learning at Work* eds D. Boud & J. Garrick, Routledge, London,
     pp. 15–28
Chi, M.T.H., Feltovich, P.J. & Glaser, R. 1981 'Categorisation and
     representation of physics problems by experts and novices'
     Cognitive Science vol. 5, pp. 121–52
Chi, M.T.H., Glaser, R. & Rees, E. 1982 'Problem-solving ability' in
     Advances in the Psychology of Human Intelligence ed. R.J. Sternberg
     vol. 1, Lawrence Erlbaum & Associates, Hillsdale, NJ, pp. 7–76
Childs, C.P. & Greenfield, P.M. 1980 'Informal modes of learning and
     teaching: The case of Zinacanteco weaving' in *Advances in Cross-
     cultural Psychology* ed. N. Warren vol. 2, Academic Press, London
Collins, A., Brown, J.S. & Newman, S.E. 1989 'Cognitive apprentice-
     ship: Teaching the crafts of reading, writing and mathematics' in
     *Knowing, Learning and Instruction: Essays in Honour of Robert
     Glaser* ed. L.B. Resnick, Lawrence Erlbaum & Associates, Hills-
     dale, NJ, pp. 453–94
Cook-Gumperez, J. & Hanna K. 1997 'Some recent issues of profes-
     sional literacy and practice' in *Changing Work, Changing Workers:
     Critical Perspectives on Language, Literacy and Skills* ed. G. Hull,
     State University of New York Press, New York, pp. 316–34
Coopers & Lybrand 1994 *TAFE NSW, Training Practices and Prefer-
     ences of Small Businesses in Australia: A Report for Vocational
     Education and Training Providers* Coopers & Lybrand, Sydney
Danford, A. 1998 'Teamworking and labour regulation in the auto-
     components industry' *Work, Employment & Society* vol. 12 no. 3,
     pp. 409–31

Darrah, C.N. 1996 *Learning and Work: An Exploration in Industrial Ethnography* Garland Publishing, New York

—— 1997 'Complicating the concept of skill requirements: Scenes from a workplace' in *Changing Work, Changing Workers: Critical Perspectives on Language, Literacy and Skills* ed. G. Hull, State University of New York Press, New York, pp. 249–72

Davis, D.D. 1995 'Form, function and strategy in boundaryless organisations' in *The Changing Nature of Work* ed. A. Howard, Jossey-Bass Publishers, San Francisco

Dewey, J. 1916 *Democracy and Education* The Free Press, New York

Dore, R.P. & Sako, M. 1989 *How the Japanese Learn to Work* Routledge, London

Dweck, C.S. & Elliott, E.S. 1983 'Achievement motivation' *Handbook of Child Psychology* vol. 4, pp. 643–91

Dweck, C.S. & Leggett, E.L. 1988 'A socio-cognitive approach to motivation and personality' *Psychological Review* vol. 95, pp. 256–73

Dymock, D. 1997 'Workplace mentoring a preliminary study' in *Good Thinking, Good Practice: Research Perspectives on Learning and Work*, 5th Annual International Conference on Post-compulsory Education and Training 26–28 November 1997, Parkroyal Surfers Paradise, Australia, vol. 2, pp. 1–12

Dymock, D. & Gerber, R. 1999 'Learning in the workplace and the classroom: An exploration,' Volume 4 of proceedings of *Changing Practice through Research and Changing Research through Practice*, 7th Annual International Conference on Post-compulsory Education and Training, pp. 84–99

Ellstrom, P.E. 1998 'The meaning of occupational competence and qualification' in *Key Qualifications in Work and Education* eds W.J. Nijhof & J.N. Streumer, Kluwer Academic Publishers, Dordrecht

Ericsson, K.A. & Simon, H.A. 1984 *Protocol Analysis—Verbal Reports as Data* MIT Press, Cambridge, MA

Evans, G. ed. 1991a *Learning and Teaching Cognitive Skills* The Australian Council for Educational Research, Melbourne

—— 1991b 'Lesson cognitive demands and student processing in upper secondary mathematics' in *Learning and Teaching Cognitive*

Skills ed. G. Evans, Australian Council for Education Research, Melbourne

—— 1993 'Institutions: formal or informal learning?' Keynote address presented at the *After Competence: The Future of Post-compulsory Education and Training* conference, Brisbane, 1–3 December

Eylon, B. & Linn, M.C. 1988 'Learning and instruction: An examination of four research perspectives in science education' *Review of Educational Research* vol. 58, pp. 251–301

Fitts, P.M. 1964 'Perceptual-motorskill learning' in *Categories of Human Learning* ed. A.W. Melton, Academic Press, New York

Forrester, K., Payne, J. & Ward, K. 1995 'Lifelong education and the workplace: A critical analysis' *International Journal of Lifelong Education* vol. 14, no. 4, pp. 292–305

Fullan, M. 1983 *The Meaning of Educational Change* Teachers Press, Columbia University, New York

—— 1985 'Change process and strategies at the local level' *Elementary School Journal* vol. 85 no. 3, pp. 391–421

Garvey, B. 1994 'Ancient Greece, MBAs, the health service and George' *Education and Training* vol. 36 no. 2, pp. 18–24

Gay, B. 1994 'What is mentoring?' *Education and Training* vol. 36 no. 5, pp. 4–7

Gimpel, J. 1983 *The Cathedral Builders* trans. T. Waugh, Pimlico, London

Glaser, R. 1984 'Education and thinking—The role of knowledge' *American Psychologist* vol. 39 no. 2, pp. 93–104

—— 1989 'Expertise and learning: How do we think about instructional processes that we have discovered knowledge structures?' in *Complex Information Processing: The Impact of Herbert A. Simon* eds D. Klahr & K. Kotovsky, Lawrence Erlbaum & Associates, Hillsdale, NJ

—— 1990 'Reemergence of learning theory within instructional research' *American Psychologist* vol. 45 no. 1, pp. 29–39

Goodnow, J.J. 1990 'The socialisation of cognition: What's involved?' in *Cultural Psychology* eds J.W. Stigler, R.A. Shweder & G. Herdt, Cambridge University Press, Cambridge, pp. 259–86

Gott, S. 1988 'Technical intuition in systems diagnosis, or accessing libraries of the mind' *Aviation, Space, and Environmental Medicine* November

—— 1989 'Apprenticeship instruction for real-world tasks: The co-ordination of procedures, mental models, and strategies' in *Review of Research in Education* ed. E.Z. Rothhopf, American Educational Research Association, Washington, DC

—— 1995 'Rediscovering learning: Acquiring expertise in real world problem-solving tasks' *Australian and New Zealand Journal of Vocational Education Research* vol. 3 no. 1, pp. 30–68

Greeno, J. 1989a 'A perspective on thinking' *American Psychologist* vol. 44 no. 2, pp. 134–41

—— 1989b 'Situations, mental models, and generative knowledge' in *Complex Information Processing: The Impact of Herbert A. Simon* eds D. Klahr & K. Kotovsky, Lawrence Erlbaum & Associates, Hillsdale, NJ

—— 1997 'On claims that answer the wrong questions' *Educational Researcher* vol. 26 no. 1, pp. 5–17

Greeno, J.G. & Simon, H.A. 1988 'Problem solving and reasoning' in *Steven's Handbook of Experimental Psychology and Education Vol. 2*, eds R.C. Aitkinson, R.J. Hormiston, G. Findeyez & R.D. Yulle, Wiley, New York

Groen, G.J. & Patel, P. 1988 'The relationship between comprehension and reasoning in medical expertise' *The Nature of Expertise* eds M.T.H. Chi, R. Glaser & R. Farr, Lawrence Erlbaum & Associates, New York

Grubb, W.N. 1996 *Working in the Middle: Strengthening Education and Training for the Mid-skilled Labor Force* Jossey-Bass, San Francisco

Hamilton, M.A. & Hamilton, S.F. 1997 'When is work a learning experience?' *Phi Delta Kappan* vol. 78 no. 9, pp. 682–9

Hamilton, S.F. 1989 'Learning on-the-job, apprentices in West Germany' *Meeting of the American Educational Research Association*, San Francisco

Harris, R. & Simons, M. 1999 'Rethinking the role of the workplace trainer: Building a learning culture', Volume 4 of proceedings of *Changing Practice Through Research and Changing Research Through Practice*, 7th Annual International Conference on Post-compulsory Education and Training, pp. 32–42

Harris, R., Simons M., Willis, P. & Underwood, F. 1996a 'You watch and then do it. They talk and you listen: On and off-job sites as learning environments', a paper presented at the Australian National Training Authority Research Advisory Council's Third Annual Conference, *Researching and Learning Together*, Melbourne, 31 October–1 November

—— 1996b 'Pandora's box or Aladdin's cave: What can on and off-job sites contribute to trainees' learning?', Vol. 2 of the proceedings of *Learning and Work: The Challenges*—4th Annual International Conference on Post-Compulsory Education and Training, pp. 7–19

Harris, L. & Volet, S. 1996 'Developing workplace learning cultures', in Vol. 2 of the proceedings of *Learning and Work: The Challenges*—4th Annual International Conference on Post-Compulsory Education and Training, pp. 83–94

—— 1997 *Developing a Learning Culture in the Workplace*, Murdoch University, Western Australia

Hodges, D.C. 1998 'Participation as dis-identification within a community of practice' *Mind, Culture and Activity* vol. 54, pp. 272–90

Hughes, K. & Bernhardt, A. 1999 *Market Segmentation and the Restructuring of Banking Jobs*, IEE Brief no. 24, February 1999, Institute on Education and the Economy, New York

Hull, G. 1997 'Preface and Introduction' *Changing Work, Changing Workers: Critical Perspectives on Language, Literacy and Skills* ed. G. Hull, State University of New York Press, New York

Hutchins, E. 1983 'Understanding Micronesian navigation' in *Mental Models* eds D. Genter & A. Stevens, Lawrence Erlbaum & Associates, Hillsdale, NJ, pp. 191–225

—— 1991 'The social organisation of distributed cognition' *Perspectives on Socially Shared Cognition* eds L.B. Resnick, J.M. Levine & S.D. Teasley, American Psychological Association, Washington, DC, pp. 283–307

—— 1993 'Learning to navigate' *Understanding Practice: Perspectives on Activity and Context* eds S. Chaiklin & J. Lave, Cambridge University Press, Cambridge, pp. 35–63

Hutchins, E. & Palen, L. 1997 'Constructing meaning from space, gesture, and speech' in *Discourse, Tools and Reasoning: Essays on Situated Cognition* eds L.B. Resnick, C. Pontecorvo, R. Saljo & B. Burge, Springer, Berlin, pp. 23–40

Jordan, B. 1989 'Cosmopolitan obstetrics: Some insights from the training of traditional midwives' *Social Science and Medicine* vol. 289, pp. 925–44

Kalusmeier, H.J. & Goodwin, W. 1975 *Learning and Human Abilities: Education Psychology* 4th edn, Harper and Row, New York

Keller, C. & Keller, J.D. 1993 'Thinking and acting with iron' in *Understanding Practice: Perspectives on Activity and Context* eds S. Chaiklin & J. Lave, Cambridge University Press, Cambridge, pp. 125–43

Kempernich, B., Butler, E. & Billett, S. 1999 *Irreconcilable Differences: Women in Small Business* National Centre for Vocational Education Research, Adelaide

Knowles, M.S. 1984 *Andragogy in Action: Applying Modern Principles of Adult Learning* Jossey-Bass, San Francisco

Larkin, J., McDermott, J., Simon, D.P. & Simon, H.A. 1980 'Expert and novice performance in solving physics problems' *Science* vol. 208, pp. 1335–42

Lave, J. 1990, 'The culture of acquisition and the practice of understanding' in *Cultural Psychology* eds J.W. Stigler, R.A. Shweder & G. Herdt, Cambridge University Press, Cambridge, pp. 259–86

—— 1991 'Situated learning in communities of practice' in *Perspectives on Socially Shared Cognition* eds L.B. Resnick, J.M. Levine and S.D. Teasley, American Psychological Association, Washington, DC, pp. 63–82

—— 1993 'The practice of learning' in *Understanding Practice: Perspectives on Activity and Context* eds S. Chaiklin & J. Lave, Cambridge University Press, Cambridge, pp. 3–32

Lave, J. & Wenger, E. 1991 *Situated Learning—Legitimate Peripheral Participation* Cambridge University Press, Cambridge

LeFevre, J.-A., Greenham, S.L. & Waheed, N. 1993 'The development of procedural and conceptual knowledge in computational estimation' *Cognition and Instruction* vol. 11 no. 2, pp. 95–132

Lesgold, A., Ivell-Friel, J. & Bonar, G. 1989 'Towards intelligent systems for testing' in *Knowing, Learning and Instruction: Essays in*

Honor of Robert Glaser ed. L.B. Resnick, Lawrence Erlbaum & Associates, Hillsdale, NJ, pp. 337–60

Lipsig-Mumme, C. 1996 'Bridging the solitudes: Canadian perspectives on Research Partnerships in the New Work Order', Keynote Address, ANTARAC Annual Conference, Melbourne, October 31–1 November

Lynch, L. 1993 *Strategies for Workplace Training: Lessons from Abroad* Economic Policy Institute, Washington, DC

Marsick, V.J. 1988 'Learning in the workplace: The case for reflectivity and critical reflectivity' *Adult Education Quarterly* vol. 38 no. 4, pp. 187–98

Marsick, V.J. & Watkins, K. 1990 *Informal and Incidental Learning in the Workplace* Routledge, London

Martin, L.M.W. & Scribner, S. 1991 'Laboratory for cognitive studies of work: A case study of the intellectual implications of a new technology' *Teachers College Record* vol. 92 no. 4, pp. 582–602

Moore, D.T. 1986 'Case studies in non-school education' *Anthropology & Education Quarterly*, vol. 17 no. 3, pp. 166–84

Miller, G.A. 1956 'The magical number seven, plus or minus two: Some limits on our capacity for processing information' *Psychological Review* vol. 63, pp. 81–97

Neiser, U. 1976 *Cognition and Reality: Principles and Implications for Cognitive Psychology* Freeman, San Francisco

Newell, A. & Simon, H.A. 1972 *Human Problem Solving* Prentice-Hall, Englewood Cliffs, NJ

Noon, M. and Blyton, P. 1997 *The Realities of Work*, Macmillan, Basingstoke

Owen, C. 1995 'Not drowning, just waving: Workplace trainers' views on perceptions of training and learning at work' *Australian and New Zealand Journal of Vocational Education Research* vol. 3 no. 1, pp. 87–109

—— 1999 'The link between organisational context and learning in the workplace: Some implications for processes of structural reform' Vol. 1 of proceedings of *Changing Practice through Research and Changing Research through Practice* 7th Annual International Conference on Post-compulsory Education and Training, pp. 95–105

Owen, E. & Sweller, J. 1989 'Should problem-solving be used as a learning device in mathematics?' *Journal of Research in Mathematics Education* vol. 20 no. 3, pp. 321–28

Pea, R.D. 1987 'Socializing the knowledge transfer problem' *International Journal of Educational Research* vol. 11 no. 6, pp. 639–63

—— 1993 'Learning scientific concepts through material and social activities: Conversational analysis meets conceptual change' *Educational Psychologist* vol. 28 no. 3, pp. 265–77

Pelissier, C. 1991 'The anthropology of teaching and learning' *Annual Review of Anthropology* vol. 20, pp. 75–95

Perkins, D., Jay, E. & Tishman, S. 1993 'Beyond abilities: A dispositional theory of thinking' *Merrill-Palmer Quarterly* vol. 39 no. 1, pp. 1–21

Piaget, J. 1966 *Psychology of Intelligence* Littlefield, Adam and Co. Totowa, NJ

—— 1976 *Behaviour and Evolution* (trans. D. Nicholson Smith) Pantheon Books, New York

Posner, G. 1982 'A cognitive science conception of curriculum and instruction' *Journal of Curriculum Studies* vol. 14, no. 4, pp. 343–51

Probert, B. 1999 'Gender workers and gendered work: Implications for women's learning' *Understanding Learning at Work* eds D. Boud & J. Garrick, Routledge, London, pp. 98–116

Prawat, R.S. 1989 'Promoting access to knowledge, strategy, and dispositions in students: A research synthesis' *Review of Educational Research* vol. 59 no. 1, pp. 1–41

—— 1993 'The value of ideas: Problems versus possibilities in learning' *Educational Researcher* vol. 22 no. 6, pp. 5–16

Raizen, S.A. 1994 'Learning and work: The research base' *Vocational Education and Training for Youth: Towards Coherent Policy and Practice*, Organisation for Economic Co-operation and Development, Paris, pp. 69–114

Resnick, L.B., Pontecorvo, C., Saljo, R. & Burge, B. 1997 'Introduction' in *Discourse, Tools and Reasoning: Essays on Situated Cognition* eds L.B. Resnick, C. Pontecorvo, R. Saljo & B. Burge, Springer, Berlin, pp. 1–20

Rogoff, B. 1982 'Integrating context and cognitive development' in

Advances in Developmental Psychology vol. 2 eds M.E. Lamb & A.L. Brown, Lawrence Erlbaum & Associates, Hillsdale, NJ, pp. 125–70

—— 1984 'Thinking and learning in social context' *Everyday Cognition: Its Development in Social Context* eds B. Rogoff & J. Lave, Harvard University Press, Cambridge, MA, pp. 1–8

—— 1990 *Apprenticeship in Thinking—Cognitive Development in Social Context* Oxford University Press, New York

—— 1995 'Observing sociocultural activities on three planes: Participatory appropriation, guided appropriation and apprenticeship' in *Sociocultural Studies of the Mind* eds J.V. Wertsch, P. Del Rio & A. Alverez, Cambridge University Press, Cambridge, pp. 139–64

Rogoff, B. & Gauvain, M. 1984 'The cognitive consequences of specific experiences—weaving versus schooling among the Navajo' *Journal of Cross-Cultural Psychology* vol. 15 no. 4, pp. 453–75

Rogoff, B. & Lave, J. eds 1984 *Everyday Cognition: Its Development in Social Context* Harvard University Press, Cambridge, MA

Rowden, R. 1995 'The role of human resources development in successful small to mid-sized manufacturing businesses: A comparative case study' *Human Resource Development Quarterly* vol. 6 no. 4, pp. 335–73

—— 1997 'How attention to employee satisfaction through training and development helps small business maintain a competitive edge: A comparative case study' *Australian Vocational Education Review* vol. 4 no. 2, pp. 33–41

Royer, J.M. 1979 'Theories of the transfer of learning' *Educational Psychologist* vol. 14, pp. 53–69

Ruddle, K. & Chesterfield, R. 1978 'Traditional skill training and labor in rural societies' *The Journal of Developing Areas* vol. 12, pp. 389–98

Ryle, G. 1949 *The Concept of Mind* Hutchinson University Library, London

Schawb, J.J. 1970 *The Practical: A Language for Curriculum* National Education Association, Center for the Study of Instruction, Washington, DC

Schoenfeld, A.H. 1985 *Mathematical Problem-solving* Academic Press, New York

Scribner, S. 1984 'Studying working intelligence' *Everyday Cognition: Its Development in Social Context* eds B. Rogoff & J. Lave, Harvard University Press, Cambridge, MA, pp. 9–40.

―――― 1985 'Vygotsky's use of history' in *Culture, Communication and Cognition: Vygotskian Perspectives* ed. J.V. Wertsch, Cambridge University Press, Cambridge, pp. 119–45

―――― 1997/1988 'Mental and manual work: An activity theory orientation' *Mind and Social Practice: Selected Writings of Sylvia Scribner* eds E. Tobah, R.J. Falmagne, M.B. Parlee, L.M. Martin & A.S. Kapelman, Cambridge University Press, Cambridge, pp. 367–74

Sefton, R. 1993 'An integrated approach to training in the vehicle industry in Australia' *Critical Forum* vol. 22, pp. 39–51

Shuell, T.J. 1990 'Phases of meaningful learning' *Review of Educational Research* vol. 60 no. 4, pp. 531–47

Simon, D.P. & Simon, H.A. 1978 'Individual differences in solving physics problems' *Children's Thinking: What Develops?* ed. R.S. Siegler, Lawrence Erlbaum & Associates, Hillsdale, NJ, pp. 236–48

Smith, A., Oczkowski, E., Noble, C. & Macklin, R. 2000 *New Management Practices and Enterprise Training* National Centre for Vocational Education Research, Adelaide

Smith, E.L., Theron, D. & Anderson, C.W. 1993 'Teaching strategies associated with conceptual change learning in science' *Journal of Research in Science Teaching* vol. 30 no. 2, pp. 11–126.

Stasz, C. & Brewer, D.J. 1999 *Academic Skills at Work: Two Perspectives* Rand Corporation, Santa Monica, California

Stasz, C. & Kaganoff, T. 1997 *Learning How to Learn at Work: Lessons from Three High School Programs* National Center for Research in Vocational Education, University of California, Berkeley

Stevenson, J.C. 1986 'Adaptability: Theoretical considerations' *Journal of Structured Learning* vol. 9, pp. 107–17

―――― 1991 'Cognitive structures for the teaching of adaptability in vocational education' in *Learning and Teaching Cognitive Skills* ed. G. Evans, Australian Council for Education Research, Melbourne, pp. 144–63

—— 1994a ed. *Cognition at Work: The Development of Vocational Expertise* National Centre for Vocational Education Research, Adelaide

—— 1994b 'Vocational Expertise' in *Cognition at Work: The Development of Vocational Expertise* ed. J. Stevenson, National Centre for Vocational Education Research, Adelaide, pp. 7–35

Stevenson, J.C. & McKavanagh, C. 1994 'Development of expertise in TAFE colleges' in *Cognition at Work: The Development of Vocational Expertise* ed. J. Stevenson, National Centre for Vocational Education Research, Adelaide, pp. 169–97

Stevenson, J.C., McKavanagh, C. & Evans, G. 1994 'Measuring the press for skill development' *Cognition at Work: The Development of Vocational Expertise* ed. J. Stevenson, National Centre for Vocational Education Research, Adelaide, pp. 198–216

Sweller, J. 1989 'Should problem solving be used as a learning device in mathematics?' *Journal of Research into Mathematics Education* vol. 20 no. 3, pp. 321–28

Tam, M. 1997 *Part-time Employment: A Bridge or a Trap?* Aldershot, Brookfield

Tennant, M. 1997 *Psychology of Adult Learning* 2nd edn, Routledge, London and New York

Tobias, S. 1994 'Interest, prior knowledge, and learning' *Review of Educational Research* vol. 64 no. 1, pp. 37–54

Van Lehn, V. 1988 'Towards a theory of impasse-driven learning' in *Learning Issues for Intelligent Tutoring Systems* eds H. Mandl & A. Lesgold, Springer-Verlag, New York, pp. 31–2

Verodonik, F., Flapan, V., Schmidt, C. & Weinstock, J. 1988 'The role of power relationships in children's cognition: Its significance for research on cognitive development' *Quarterly Newsletter of the Laboratory of Comparative Human Cognition* vol. 10, pp. 80–85

von Glasersfeld, E. 1987 'Learning as a constructive activity' *Problems of Representation in the Teaching and Learning of Mathematics* ed. C. Janvier, Lawrence Erlbaum & Associates, Hillsdale, NJ

Valsiner, J. 1994 'Bi-directional cultural transmission and constructive sociogenesis' in *Sociogenesis Re-examined* eds W. de Graaf & R. Maier, Springer, New York, pp. 101–34

Volkoff, V. 1996 'A shared endeavour: The role of mentors in work-based professional development', vol. 2 of the proceedings of

Learning and Work: The Challenges—4th Annual International Conference on Post-Compulsory Education and Training, pp. 71–82

Voss, J.F., Tyler, S. & Yengo, L. 1983 'Individual differences in the solving of social science problems' *Individual Differences in Problem-solving* eds R. Dillion & R. Schmeck, Academic Press, San Diego

Vygotsky, L.S. 1978 *Mind in Society—The Development of Higher Psychological Processes* Harvard University Press, Cambridge

Wall, T.D. & Jackson, P.R. 1995 'New manufacturing initiatives and shopfloor job design' in *The Changing Nature of Work* ed. A. Howard, Jossey-Bass, San Francisco

Wenger, E. 1998 *Communities of Practice: Learning, Meaning, and Identity* Cambridge University Press, Cambridge

Wertsch, J.W. 1998 *Mind as Action* Oxford University Press, New York

Whalley, P. & Barley, S.R. 1997 'Technical work in the division of labor: Stalking the wily anomaly' in *Between Craft and Science: Technical Work in U.S. Settings* eds S.R. Barley & J.E. Orr, Cornell University Press, Ithaca, NY, pp. 24–52

Zuboff, S. 1988 *In the Age of the Smart Machine: The Future of Work and Power* Basic Books, New York

Index